BEETHOVEN

THE MAN AND THE ARTIST, AS REVEALED IN HIS OWN WORDS

BEETHOVEN

THE MAN AND THE ARTIST, AS REVEALED IN HIS OWN WORDS

Compiled and Annotated by
FRIEDRICH KERST

Translated into English, and Edited,
with Additional Notes, by
HENRY EDWARD KREHBIEL

DOVER PUBLICATIONS, INC.
NEW YORK

This Dover edition, first published in 1964, is an unabridged and unaltered republication of the work first published by B. W. Huebsch in 1905.

International Standard Book Number: 0-486-21261-0

Library of Congress Catalog Card Number: 64-18854

Manufactured in the United States of America

Dover Publications, Inc.
180 Varick Street
New York 14, N.Y.

CONTENTS

PREFACE

This little book came into existence as if it
were by chance. The author had devoted himself for a long time to the study of Beethoven
and carefully scrutinized all manner of books,
publications, manuscripts, etc., in order to de-
rive the greatest possible information about the
hero. He can say confidently that he conned
every existing publication of value. His notes
made during his readings grew voluminous, and
also his amazement at the wealth of Beethoven's
observations comparatively unknown to his admirers because hidden away, like concealed vio-
lets, in books which have been long out of print
and for whose reproduction there is no urgent
call. These observations are of the utmost im-
portance for the understanding of Beethoven
in whom man and artist are inseparably united.
Within the pages of this little book are included all of them which seemed to possess value,
either as expressions of universal truths or as
evidence of the character of Beethoven or his
compositions.

Beethoven is brought more directly before our
knowledge by these his own words than by the
diffuse books which have been written about him.
For this reason the compiler has added only the
necessary explanatory notes, and (on the ad-

vice of professional friends) the remarks introductory to the various subdivisions of the book.
He dispensed with a biographical introduction;
there are plenty of succinct biographies, which
set forth the circumstances of the master's life
easily to be had. Those who wish to penetrate
farther into the subject would do well to read
the great work by Thayer, the foundation of
all Beethoven biography (in the new revision
now making by Deiters), or the critical biography by Marx, as revised by Behncke. In sift-
ing the material it was found that it fell naturally into thirteen subdivisions. In arranging
the succession of utterances care was had to
group related subjects. By this means unnecessary interruptions in the train of thought were
avoided and interesting comparisons made possible. To this end it was important that time,
place and circumstances of every word should
be conscientiously set down.

Concerning the selection of material let it be
said that in all cases of doubt the authenticity
of every utterance was proved; Beethoven is
easily recognizable in the form and contents of
his sayings. Attention must be directed to two
matters in particular: after considerable reflection the compiler decided to include in the collection a few quotations which Beethoven copied
from books which he read. From the fact that
he took the trouble to write them down, we may
assume that they had a fascination for him, and
were greeted with lively emotion as being admi-

rable expressions of thoughts which had moved
him. They are very few, and the fact that they
are quotations is plainly indicated. By copying
them into his note-books Beethoven as much as
stored them away in the thesaurus of his
thoughts, and so they may well have a place
here. A word touching the use of the three
famous letters to Bettina von Arnim, the peculiarities of which differentiate them from the entire mass of Beethoven's correspondence and
compel an inquiry into their genuineness: As a
correspondent Bettina von Arnim has a poor
reputation since the discovery of her pretty for-
gery, " Goethes Briefwechsel mit einem Kinde "
(Goethe's Correspondence with a Child). In
this alleged " Correspondence " she made use of
fragmentary material which was genuine, pieced
it out with her own inventions, and even went
so far as to turn into letters poems written by
Goethe to her and other women. The genuineness of a poem by Beethoven to Bettina is in-
dubitable ; it will be found in the chapter entitled
" Concerning Texts." Doubt was thrown on
the letters immediately on their appearance in
1839. Bettina could have dissipated all suspi-
cion had she produced the originals ; she remained silent. One letter, however, that dated
February 10, 1811, afterward came to light.
Bettina had given it to Philipp von Nathusius.
It had always been thought the most likely one
of the set to be authentic ; the compiler has,
therefore, used it without hesitation. From the

other letters, in which a mixture of the genuine and the fictitious must be assumed so long as the originals are not produced, passages have been taken which might have been thus constructed by Beethoven. On the contrary, the voluminous communications of Bettina to Goethe, in which she relates her conversations with Beethoven, were scarcely used. It is significant, so far as these are concerned, that, according to Bettina's own statement, when she read the letter to him before sending it off, Beethoven cried out, " Did I really say that? If so I must have had a *raptus*."

In conclusion the compiler directs attention to the fact that in a few cases utterances which have been transmitted to us only in an indirect form have been altered to present them in a direct form, inasmuch as their contents seemed too valuable to omit simply because their production involved a trifling change in form.

Elberfeld, October, 1904.   Fr. K.

CONCERNING ART

Beethoven's relation to art might almost be described as personal. Art was his goddess to whom he made petition, to whom he rendered thanks, whom he defended. He praised her as his savior in times of despair; by his own confession it was only the prospect of her comforts that prevented him from laying violent hands on himself. Read his words and you shall find that it was his art that was his companion in his wanderings through field and forest, the sharer of the solitude to which his deafness condemned him. The concepts Nature and Art were intimately bound up in his mind. His lofty and idealistic conception of art led him to proclaim the purity of his goddess with the hot zeal of a priestly fanatic. Every form of pseudo or bastard art stirred him with hatred to the bottom of his soul; hence his furious onslaughts on mere virtuosity and all efforts from influential sources to utilize art for other than purely artistic purposes. And his art rewarded his devotion richly; she made his sorrowful life worth living with gifts of purest joy.

[" To Beethoven music was not only a manifestation of the beautiful, an art, it was akin to religion. He felt himself to be a prophet, a seer. All the misanthropy engendered by his unhappy relations with mankind, could not shake his devotion to this ideal which had sprung

from truest artistic apprehension and been nurtured by
enforced introspection and philosophic reflection." "Music and Manners," page 237. H. E. K.]

1. 'Tis said, that art is long, and life but
      fleeting:—
   Nay; life is long, and brief the span
      of art;
   If e'er her breath vouchsafes with gods a
      meeting,
   A moment's favor 'tis of which we've
      had a part.
   Conversation book, March, 1820. Probably a quotation.

2. The world is a king, and, like a king, desires flattery in return for favor; but true art
is selfish and perverse—it will not submit to the
mould of flattery.

   Conversation book, March, 1820. When Baron von
Braun expressed the opinion that the opera "Fidelio"
would eventually win the enthusiasm of the upper tiers,
Beethoven said: "I do not write for the galleries!" He
never permitted himself to be persuaded to make conces-
sions to the taste of the masses.

3. Continue to translate yourself to the
heaven of art; there is no more undisturbed, un-
mixed, purer happiness than may thus be attained.

   August 19, 1817, to Xaver Schnyder, who vainly sought
instruction from Beethoven in 1811, though he was pleas-
antly received.

4. Go on; do not practise art alone but penetrate to her heart; she deserves it, for art and
science only can raise man to godhood.

Teplitz, July 17, 1812, to his ten years' old admirer, Emilie M. in H.

5. True art is imperishable and the true artist finds profound delight in grand productions of genius.

March 15, 1823, to Cherubini, to whom he also wrote: " I prize your works more than all others written for the stage." The letter asks Cherubini to interest himself in obtaining a subscription from King Louis XVIII for the Solemn Mass in D. [Cherubini declared that he had never received the letter. That it was not only the hope of obtaining a favor which prompted Beethoven to express so high an admiration for Cherubini, is plain from a remark made by the English musician Cipriani Potter to A. W. Thayer in 1861. I found it in Thayer's notebooks which were placed in my hands for examination after his death. One day Potter asked, " Who is the greatest living composer, yourself excepted? " Beethoven seemed puzzled for a moment, and then exclaimed, " Cherubini." H. E. K.]

6. Truth exists for the wise; beauty for the susceptible heart. They belong together—are complementary.

Written in the autograph book of his friend, Lenz von Breuning, in 1797.

7. When I open my eyes, a sigh involuntarily escapes me, for all that I see runs counter to my religion; perforce I despise the world which does not intuitively feel that music is a higher revelation than all wisdom and philosophy.

Remark made to Bettina von Arnim, in 1810, concerning Vienna society. Report in a letter by Bettina to Goethe on May 28, 1810.

8. Art! Who comprehends her? With whom can one consult concerning this great goddess?

August 11, 1810, to Bettina von Arnim.

9. In the country I know no lovelier delight than quartet music.

To Archduke Rudolph, in a letter addressed to Baden on July 24, 1813.

10. Nothing but art, cut to form like old old-fashioned hoop-skirts. I never feel entirely well except when I am among scenes of unspoiled nature.

September 24, 1826, to Breuning, while promenading with Breuning's family in the Schönbrunner Garden, after calling attention to the alleys of trees "trimmed like walls, in the French manner."

11. Nature knows no quiescence; and true art walks with her hand in hand; her sister, from whom heaven forefend us! is called artificiality.

From notes in the lesson book of Archduke Rudolph, following some remarks on the expansion of the expressive capacity of music.

LOVE OF NATURE

Beethoven was a true son of the Rhine in his love for nature. As a boy he had taken extended trips, sometimes occupying days, with his father " through the Rhenish localities everlastingly dear to me." In his days of physical health Nature was his instructress in art; " I may not come without my banner," he used to say when he set out upon his wanderings even in his latest years, and never without his notebooks. In the scenes of nature he found his marvellous motives and themes; brook, birds and tree sang to him. In a few special cases he has himself recorded the fact.

But when he was excluded more and more from communion with his fellow men because of his increasing deafness, until, finally, he could communicate only by writing with others (hence the Conversation-books, which will be cited often in this little volume), he fled for refuge to nature. Out in the woods he again became naïvely happy; to him the woods were a Holy of Holies, a Home of the Mysteries. Forest and mountain-vale heard his sighs; there he unburdened his heavy-laden heart. When his friends need comfort he recommends a retreat to nature. Nearly every summer he leaves hot and dusty Vienna and seeks a quiet spot in the beautiful

15

neighborhood. To call a retired and reposeful little spot his own is his burning desire.

12. On the Kahlenberg, 1812, end of September.

Almighty One	O God!
In the woods	What glory in the
I am blessed.	Woodland.
Happy every one	On the Heights
In the woods.	is Peace,—
Every tree speaks	Peace to serve
Through Thee.	Him—

This poetic exclamation, accompanied by a few notes, is on a page of music paper owned by Joseph Joachim.

13. How happy I am to be able to wander among bushes and herbs, under trees and over rocks; no man can love the country as I love it. Woods, trees and rocks send back the echo that man desires.

To Baroness von Drossdick.

14. O God! send your glance into beautiful nature and comfort your moody thoughts touching that which must be.

To the " Immortal Beloved," July 6, in the morning. [Thayer has spoiled the story so long believed, and still spooking in the books of careless writers, that the " Immortal Beloved " was the Countess Giulietta Guicciardi, to whom the C-sharp minor sonata is dedicated. The real person to whom the love-letters were addressed was the Countess Brunswick to whom Beethoven was engaged to be married when he composed the fourth Symphony. H. E. K.]

15. My miserable hearing does not trouble me here. In the country it seems as if every tree said to me: "Holy! holy!"—Who can give complete expression to the esctasy of the woods! O, the sweet stillness of the woods!

July, 1814; he had gone to Baden after the benefit performance of " Fidelio."

16. My fatherland, the beautiful locality in which I saw the light of the world, appears before me vividly and just as beautiful as when I left you; I shall count it the happiest experience of my life when I shall again be able to see you, and greet our Father Rhine.

Vienna, June 29, to Wegeler, in Bonn. In 1825 Beethoven said to his pupil Ries, " Fare well in the Rhine country which is ever dear to me," and in 1826 wrote to Schott, the publisher in Mayence, about the " Rhine country which I so long to see again."

17. Brühl, at " The Lamb "—how lovely to see my native country again!

Diary, 1812-1818.

18. A little house here, so small as to yield one's self a little room,—only a few days in this divine Brühl,—longing or desire, emancipation or fulfillment.

Written in 1816 in Brühl near Mödling among the sketches for the Scherzo of the pianoforte sonata op. 106. [Like many another ejaculatory remark of Beethoven's difficult to understand. See Appendix. H. E. K.]

19. When you reach the old ruins, think that Beethoven often paused there; if you wander through the mysterious fir forests, think that

Beethoven often poetized, or, as is said, composed there.

In the fall of 1817, to Mme. Streicher, who was at a cure in Baden.

20. Nature is a glorious school for the heart! 'Tis well; I shall be a scholar in this school and bring an eager heart to her instruction. Here I shall learn wisdom, the only wisdom that is free from disgust; here I shall learn to know God and find a foretaste of heaven in His knowledge. Among these occupations my earthly days shall flow peacefully along until I am accepted into that world where I shall no longer be a student, but a knower of wisdom.

Copied into his diary, in 1818, from Sturm's " Betrachtungen über die Werke Gottes in der Natur."

21. Soon autumn will be here. Then I wish to be like unto a fruitful tree which pours rich stores of fruit into our laps! But in the winter of existence, when I shall be gray and sated with life, I desire for myself the good fortune that my repose be as honorable and beneficent as the repose of nature in the winter time.

Copied from the same work of Sturm's.

CONCERNING TEXTS

Not even a Beethoven was spared the tormenting question of texts for composition. It is fortunate for posterity that he did not exhaust his energies in setting inefficient libretti, that he did not believe that good music would suffice to command success in spite of bad texts. The majority of his works belong to the field of purely instrumental music. Beethoven often gave expression to the belief that words were a less capable medium of proclamation for feelings than music. Nevertheless it may be observed that he looked upon an opera, or lyric drama, as the crowning work of his life. He was in communication with the best poets of his time concerning opera texts. A letter of his on the subject was found in the blood-spotted pocketbook of Theodor Körner. The conclusion of his creative labors was to be a setting of Goethe's " Faust; " except " Fidelio," however, he gave us no opera. His songs are not many although he sought carefully for appropriate texts. Unhappily the gift of poetry was not vouchsafed him.

22. Always the same old story: the Germans can not put together a good libretto.

To C. M. von Weber, concerning the book of " Euryanthe," at Baden, in October, 1823. Mozart said: "Verses are the most indispensable thing for music, but rhymes, for the sake of rhymes, the most injurious. Those who go to work so pedantically will assuredly come to grief, along with the music."

23. It is difficult to find a good poem. Grillparzer has promised to write one for me,—indeed, he has already written one; but we can not understand each other. I want something entirely different than he.

In the spring of 1825, to Ludwig Rellstab, who was intending to write an opera-book for Beethoven. It may not be amiss to recall the fact that Mozart examined over one hundred librettos, according to his own statement, before he decided to compose "The Marriage of Figaro."

24. It is the duty of every composer to be familiar with all poets, old and new, and himself choose the best and most fitting for his purposes.

In a recommendation of Kandler's "Anthology."

25. The genre would give me little concern provided the subject were attractive to me. It must be such that I can go to work on it with love and ardor. I could not compose operas like "Don Juan" and "Figaro;" toward them I feel too great a repugnance. I could never have chosen such subjects; they are too frivolous.

In the spring of 1825, to Ludwig Rellstab.

26. I need a text which stimulates me; it must be something moral, uplifting. Texts such as Mozart composed I should never have been able to set to music. I could never have got myself into a mood for licentious texts. I have

received many librettos, but, as I have said, none that met my wishes.

To young Gerhard von Breuning.

27. I know the text is extremely bad, but after one has conceived an entity out of even a bad text, it is difficult to make changes in details without disturbing the unity. If it is a single word, on which occasionally great weight is laid, it must be permitted to stand. He is a bad author who can not, or will not try to make something as good as possible; if this is not the case petty changes will certainly not improve the whole.

Teplitz, August 23, 1811, to Härtel, the publisher, who wanted some changes made in the book of "The Mount of Olives."

28. Good heavens! Do they think in Saxony that the words make good music? If an inappropriate word can spoil the music, which is true, then we ought to be glad when we find that words and music are one and not try to improve matters even if the verbal expression is commonplace—*dixi*.

January 28, to Gottfried Härtel, who had undertaken to make changes in the book of "The Mount of Olives" despite the prohibition of Beethoven.

29. Goethe's poems exert a great power over me not only because of their contents but also because of their rhythms; I am stimulated to compose by this language, which builds itself up

to higher orders as if through spiritual agencies,
and bears in itself the secret of harmonies.

Reported as an expression of Beethoven's by Bettina
von Arnim to Goethe.

30. Schiller's poems are difficult to set to
music. The composer must be able to rise far
above the poet. Who can do that in the case
of Schiller? In this respect Goethe is much
easier.

1809, after Beethoven had made his experiences with
the " Hymn to Joy " and " Egmont."

ON COMPOSING

Wiseacres not infrequently accused Beethoven of want of regularity in his compositions. In various ways and at divers times he gave vigorous utterance to his opinions of such pedantry. He was not the most tractable of pupils, especially in Vienna, where, although he was highly praised as a player, he took lessons in counterpoint from Albrechtsberger. He did not endure long with Papa Haydn. He detested the study of fugue in particular; the fugue was to him a symbol of narrow coercion which choked all emotion. Mere formal beauty, moreover, was nothing to him. Over and over again he emphasizes soul, feeling, direct and immediate life, as the first necessity of an art work. It is therefore not strange that under certain circumstances he ignored conventional forms in sonata and symphony. An irrepressible impulse toward freedom is the most prominent peculiarity of the man and artist Beethoven; nearly all of his observations, no matter what their subject, radiate the word " Liberty." In his remarks about composing there. is a complete exposition of his method of work.

31. As regards me, great heavens! my do-

minion is in the air; the tones whirl like the
wind, and often there is a like whirl in my soul.
February 13, 1814, to Count Brunswick, in Buda.

32. Then the loveliest themes slipped out of
your eyes into my heart, themes which shall only
then delight the world when Beethoven conducts
no longer.
August 15, 1812, to Bettina von Arnim.

33. I always have a picture in my mind when
composing, and follow its lines.

In 1815, to Neate, while promenading with him in
Baden and talking about the "Pastoral" symphony.
Ries relates: "While composing Beethoven frequently
thought of an object, although he often laughed at musical delineation and scolded about petty things of the
sort. In this respect 'The Creation' and 'The Seasons' were many times a butt, though without depreciation of Haydn's loftier merits. Haydn's choruses and
other works were loudly praised by Beethoven."

34. The texts which you sent me are least of
all fitted for song. The description of a picture
belongs to the field of painting; in this the poet
can count himself more fortunate than my muse
for his territory is not so restricted as mine in
this respect, though mine, on the other hand, ex-
tends into other regions, and my dominion is not
easily reached.

Nussdorf, July 15, 1817, to Wilhelm Gerhard, who
had sent him some Anacreontic songs for composition.

35. Carried too far, all delineation in instrumental music loses in efficiency.

A remark in the sketches for the "Pastoral" symphony, preserved in the Royal Library in Berlin. Mozart

said: " Even in the most terrifying moments music must never offend the ear."

36. Yes, yes, then they are amazed and put their heads together because they never found it in any book on thorough bass.

To Ries when the critics accused him of making grammatical blunders in music.

37. No devil can compel me to write only cadences of such a kind.

From notes written in his years of study. Beethoven called the composition of fugues " the art of making musical skeletons."

38. Good singing was my guide; I strove to write as flowingly as possible and trusted in my ability to justify myself before the judgment-seat of sound reason and pure taste.

From notes in the instruction book of Archduke Rudolph.

39. Does he believe that I think of a wretched fiddle when the spirit speaks to me?

To his friend, the admirable violinist Schuppanzigh, when the latter complained of the difficulty of a passage in one of his works. [Beethoven here addresses his friend in the third person, which is the customary style of address for the German nobility and others towards inferiors in rank. H. E. K.]

40. The Scotch songs show how unconstrainedly irregular melodies can be treated with the help of harmony.

Diary, 1812-1818. Since 1809 Beethoven had arranged Folk-songs for Thomson of Edinburgh.

41. To write true church music, look through the old monkish chorals, etc., also the most correct translations of the periods, and perfect prosody in the Catholic Psalms and hymns generally.

Diary, 1818.

42. Many assert that every minor piece must end in the minor. *Nego!* On the contrary I find that in the soft scales the major third at the close has a glorious and uncommonly quieting effect. Joy follows sorrow, sunshine—rain. It affects me as if I were looking up to the silvery glistering of the evening star.

From Archduke Rudolph's book of instruction.

43. Rigorists, and devotees of antiquity, relegate the perfect fourth to the list of dissonances. Tastes differ. To my ear it gives not the least offence combined with other tones.

From Archduke Rudolph's book of instruction, compiled in 1809.

44. When the gentlemen can think of nothing new, and can go no further, they quickly call in a diminished seventh chord to help them out of the predicament.

A remark made to Schindler.

45. My dear boy, the startling effects which many credit to the natural genius of the composer, are often achieved with the greatest ease by the use and resolution of the diminished seventh chords.

Reported by Karl Friederich Hirsch, a pupil of Beethoven in the winter of 1816. He was a grandson of Albrechtsberger who had given lessons to Beethoven.

46. In order to become a capable composer one must have already learned harmony and counterpoint at the age of from seven to eleven years, so that when the fancy and emotions awake one shall know what to do according to the rules.

Reported by Schindler as having been put into the mouth of Beethoven by a newspaper of Vienna. Schindler says: "When Beethoven came to Vienna he knew no counterpoint, and little harmony."

47. So far as mistakes are concerned it was never necessary for me to learn thorough-bass; my feelings were so sensitive from childhood that I practised counterpoint without knowing that it must be so or could be otherwise.

Note on a sheet containing directions for the use of fourths in suspensions—probably intended for the instruction of Archduke Rudolph.

48. Continue, Your Royal Highness, to write down briefly your occasional ideas while at the pianoforte. For this a little table alongside the pianoforte is necessary. By this means not only is the fancy strengthened, but one learns to hold fast in a moment the most remote conceptions. It is also necessary to compose without the pianoforte; say often a simple chord melody, with simple harmonies, then figurate according to the rules of counterpoint, and beyond them; this will give Y. R. H. no headache, but, on the contrary, feeling yourself thus in the midst of art, a great pleasure.

July 1, 1823, to his pupil Archduke Rudolph.

49. The bad habit, which has clung to me from childhood, of always writing down a musical thought which occurs to me, good or bad, has often been harmful to me.

July 23, 1815, to Archduke Rudolph, while excusing himself for not having visited H. R. H., on the ground that he had been occupied in noting a musical idea which had occurred to him.

50. As is my habit, the pianoforte part of the concerto (op. 19) was not written out in the score; I have just written it, wherefore, in order to expedite matters, you receive it in my not too legible handwriting.

April 22, 1801, to the publisher Hofmeister, in Leipsic.

51. Correspondence, as you know, was never my forte; some of my best friends have not had a letter from me in years. I live only in my notes (compositions), and one is scarcely finished when another is begun. As I am working now I often compose three, even four, pieces simultaneously.

Vienna, June 29, 1800, to Wegeler, in Bonn.

52. I never write a work continuously, without interruption. I am always working on several at the same time, taking up one, then another.

June 1, 1816, to Medical Inspector Dr. Karl von Bursy, when the latter asked about an opera (the book by Berge, sent to Beethoven by Amenda), which was never written.

53. I must accustom myself to think out at once the whole, as soon as it shows itself, with all the voices, in my head.

[Note in a sketch-book of 1810, containing studies for

the music to " Egmont " and the great Trio in B-flat, op. 97. H. E. K.]

54. I carry my thoughts about me for a long time, often a very long time, before I write them down; meanwhile my memory is so faithful that I am sure never to forget, not even in years, a theme that has once occurred to me. I change many things, discard, and try again until I am satisfied. Then, however, there begins in my head the development in every direction, and, inasmuch as I know exactly what I want, the fundamental idea never deserts me,—it arises before me, grows,—I see and hear the picture in all its extent and dimensions stand before my mind like a cast, and there remains for me nothing but the labor of writing it down, which is quickly accomplished when I have the time, for I sometimes take up other work, but never to the confusion of one with the other. You will ask me where I get my ideas. That I can not tell you with certainty; they come unsummoned, directly, indirectly,—I could seize them with my hands,—out in the open air; in the woods; while walking; in the silence of the nights; early in the morning; incited by moods, which are translated by the poet into words, by me into tones that sound, and roar and storm about me until I have set them down in notes.

Said to Louis Schlösser, a young musician, whom Beethoven honored with his friendship in 1822-23.

55. On the whole the carrying out of several

voices in strict relationship mutually hinders
their progress.

Fall of 1812, in the Diary of 1812-18.

56. Few as are the claims which I make upon
such things I shall still accept the dedication of
your beautiful work with pleasure. You ask,
however, that I also play the part of a critic,
without thinking that I must myself submit to
criticism! With Voltaire I believe that " a few
fly-bites can not stop a spirited horse." In this
respect I beg of you to follow my example. In
order not to approach you surreptitiously, but
openly as always, I say that in future works
of the character you might give more heed to
the individualization of the voices.

Vienna, May 10, 1826. To whom the letter was sent
is not known, though from the manner of address it is
plain that he was of the nobility.

57. Your variations show talent, but I must
fault you for having changed the theme. Why?
What man loves must not be taken away from
him;—moreover to do this is to make changes
before variations.

Baden, July 6, 1804, to Wiedebein, a teacher of music
in Brunswick.

58. I am not in the habit of rewriting my
compositions. I never did it because I am pro-
foundly convinced that every change of detail
changes the character of the whole.

February 19, 1813, to George Thomson, who had re-
quested some changes in compositions submitted to him
for publication.

59. One must not hold one's self so divine as to be unwilling occasionally to make improvements in one's creations.

March 4, 1809, to Breitkopf and Härtel, when indicating a few changes which he wished to have made in the symphonies op. 67 and 68.

60. The unnatural rage for transcribing pianoforte pieces for string instruments (instruments that are in every respect so different from each other) ought to end. I stoutly maintain that only Mozart could have transcribed his own works,—and Haydn; and without putting myself on a level with these great men I assert the same thing about my pianoforte sonatas. Not only must entire passages be elided and changed, but additions must be made; and right here lies the rock of offence to overcome which one must be the master of himself or be possessed of the same skill and inventiveness.—I transcribed but a single sonata for string quartet, and I am sure that no one will easily do it after me.

July 13, 1802, in an announcement of several compositions, among them the quintet op. 29.

61. Were it not that my income brings in nothing, I should compose nothing but grand symphonies, church music, or, at the outside, quartets in addition.

December 20, 1822, to Peters, publisher, in Leipsic. His income had been reduced from 4,000 to 800 florins by depreciation of the Austrian money. [There is in the original one of the puns which Beethoven was fond of making: " Wäre mein Gehalt nicht gänzlich ohne Gehalt." H. E. K.]

ON PERFORMING MUSIC

While reading Beethoven's views on the subject of how music ought to be performed, it is but natural to inquire about his own manner of playing. On this point Ries, his best pupil, reports: " In general Beethoven played his own compositions very capriciously, yet he adhered, on the whole, strictly to the beat and only at times, but seldom, accelerated the *tempo* a trifle. Occasionally he would retard the *tempo* in a *crescendo,* which produced a very beautiful and striking effect. While playing he would give a passage, now in the right hand, now in the left, a beautiful expression which was simply inimitable; but it was rarely indeed that he added a note or an ornament." Of his playing when still a young man one of his hearers said that it was in the slow movements particularly that it charmed everybody. Almost unanimously his contemporaries give him the palm for his improvisations. Ries says: " His extemporizations were the most extraordinary things that one could hear. No artist that I ever heard came at all near the height which Beethoven attained. The wealth of ideas which forced themselves on him, the caprices to which he surrendered himself, the variety of treatment, the difficulties, were inexhaustible." His playing was not technically perfect. He let many a note " fall under the table," but without marring the effect of his playing. Concerning this we have a remark of his own in No. 75. Somewhat critical is Czerny's report: " Extraordinary as his extempore playing was it was less successful in the performance of printed compositions; for, since he never took the time or had the patience to practise anything, his success depended mostly on chance and mood; and since, also, his manner of playing as well as composing was ahead of his time, the weak and imperfect pianofortes of his time could not withstand his gigantic style. It was because of this that Hummel's purling and brilliant manner of play, well adapted to the period, was more intelligible and attractive to the great public. But Beethoven's playing in *adagios* and *legato*, in the sustained style, made an almost magical impression on every hearer, and, so far as I know, it has never been surpassed." Czerny's remark about the pianofortes of Beethoven's day explains Beethoven's judgment on his own pianoforte sonatas. He composed for the sonorous pianoforte of the future,—the pianoforte building to-day.

The following anecdote, told by Czerny, will be read with pleasure. Pleyel, a famous musician, came to Vienna from Paris in 1805, and had his latest quartets performed in the palace of Prince Lobkowitz. Beethoven was present and was asked to play something. " As usual, he submitted to the interminable entreaties and

finally was dragged almost by force to the pianoforte by the ladies. Angrily he tears the
second violin part of one of the Pleyel quartets
from the music-stand where it still lay open,
throws it upon the rack of the pianoforte, and
begins to improvise. We had never heard him
extemporize more brilliantly, with more origi-
nality or more grandly than on that evening.
But throughout the entire improvisation there
ran in the middle voices, like a thread, or *cantus
firmus*, the insignificant notes, wholly insignificant in themselves, which he found on the page
of the quartet, which by chance lay open on
the music-stand; on them he built up the most
daring melodies and harmonies, in the most brilliant concert style. Old Pleyel could only give
expression to his amazement by kissing his
hands. After such improvisations Beethoven
was wont to break out into a loud and satisfied
laugh." Czerny says further of his playing:
" In rapidity of scale passages, trills, leaps,
etc., no one equalled him,—not even Hummel.
His attitude at the pianoforte was perfectly
quiet and dignified, with no approach to grim-
ace, except to bend down a little towards the keys
as his deafness increased; his fingers were very
powerful, not long, and broadened at the tips
by much playing; for he told me often that in
his youth he had practised stupendously, mostly
till past midnight. In teaching he laid great
stress on a correct position of the fingers (according to the Emanuel Bach method, in which

he instructed me) ; he himself could barely span
a tenth. He made frequent use of the pedal,
much more frequently than is indicated in his
compositions. His reading of the scores of
Händel and Gluck and the fugues of Bach was
unique, inasmuch as he put a polyphony and
spirit into the former which gave the works a
new form."

In his later years the deaf master could no
longer hear his own playing which therefore
came to have a pitifully painful effect. Concerning his manner of conducting, Seyfried
says: " It would no wise do to make our master
a model in conducting, and the orchestra had to
take great care lest it be led astray by its men-
tor; for he had an eye only for his composition
and strove unceasingly by means of manifold
gesticulations to bring out the expression which
he desired. Often when he reached a *forte* he
gave a violent down beat even if the note were
an unaccented one. He was in the habit of
marking a *diminuendo* by crouching down lower
and lower, and at a *pianissimo* he almost crept
under the stand. With a *crescendo* he, too, grew,
rising as if out of a stage trap, and with the
entrance of a *fortissimo* he stood on his toes and
seemed to take on gigantic proportions, while
he waved his arms about as if trying to soar
upwards to the clouds. Everything about him
was in activity; not a part of his organization
remained idle, and the whole man seemed like a
perpetuum mobile. Concerning expression, the

little nuances, the equable division of light and shade, as also an effective *tempo rubato*, he was extremely exact and gladly discussed them with the individual members of the orchestra without showing vexation or anger."

62. It has always been known that the greatest pianoforte players were also the greatest composers; but how did they play? Not like the pianists of to-day who prance up and down the key-board with passages in which they have exercised themselves,—*putsch, putsch, putsch;* —what does that mean? Nothing. When the true pianoforte virtuosi played it was always something homogeneous, an entity; it could be transcribed and then it appeared as a well-thought-out work. That is pianoforte playing; the other is nothing!

In conversation with Tomaschek, October, 1814.

63. Candidly I am not a friend of *Allegri di bravura* and such, since they do nothing but promote mechanism.

Hetzendorf, July 16, 1823, to Ries in London.

64. The great pianists have nothing but technique and affectation.

Fall of 1817, to Marie Pachler-Koschak, a pianist whom Beethoven regarded very highly. "You will play the sonatas in F major and C minor, for me, will you not?"

65. As a rule, in the case of these gentlemen,

all reason and feeling are generally lost in the nimbleness of their fingers.

Reported by Schindler as a remark of Beethoven's concerning pianoforte virtuosi.

66. Habit may depreciate the most brilliant talents.

In 1812, to his pupil, Archduke Rudolph, whom he warns against too zealous a devotion to music.

67. You will have to play a long time yet before you realize that you can not play at all.

July, 1808. Reported by Rust as having been said to a young man who played for Beethoven.

68. One must be something if one wishes to put on appearances.

August 15, 1812, to Bettina von Arnim.

69. These pianoforte players have their coteries whom they often join; there they are praised continually,—and there's an end of art!

Conversation with Tomaschek, October, 1814.

70. We Germans have too few dramatically trained singers for the part of *Leonore*. They are too cold and unfeeling; the Italians sing and act with body and soul.

1824, in Baden, to Freudenberg, an organist from Breslau.

71. If he is a master of his instrument I rank an organist amongst the first of virtuosi. I too, played the organ a great deal when I was young, but my nerves would not stand the power of the gigantic instrument.

To Freudenberg, in Baden.

72. I never wrote noisy music. For my instrumental works I need an orchestra of about sixty good musicians. I am convinced that only such a number can bring out the quickly changing graduations in performance.

Reported by Schindler.

73. A Requiem ought to be quiet music,—it needs no trump of doom; memories of the dead require no hubbub.

Reported by Holz to Fanny von Ponsing, in Baden, summer of 1858. According to the same authority Beethoven valued Cherubini's "Requiem" more highly than any other.

74. No metronome at all! He who has sound feeling needs none, and he who has not will get no help from the metronome;—he'll run away with the orchestra anyway.

Reported by Schindler. It had been found that Beethoven himself had sent different metronomic indications to the publisher and the Philharmonic Society of London.

75. In reading rapidly a multitude of misprints may pass unnoticed because you are familiar with the language.

To Wegeler, who had expressed wonder at Beethoven's rapid *prima vista* playing, when it was impossible to see each individual note.

76. The poet writes his monologue or dialogue in a certain, continuous rhythm, but the elocutionist in order to insure an understanding of the sense of the lines, must make pauses and interruptions at places where the poet was not permitted to indicate it by punctuation.

The same manner of declamation can be applied to music, and admits of modification only according to the number of performers.

Reported by Schindler, Beethoven's faithful factotum.

77. With respect to his playing with you, when he has acquired the proper mode of fingering and plays in time and plays the notes with tolerable correctness, only then direct his attention to the matter of interpretation; and when he has gotten this far do not stop him for little mistakes, but point them out at the end of the piece. Although I have myself given very little instruction I have always followed this method which quickly makes *musicians*, and that, after all, is one of the first objects of art.

To Czerny, who was teaching music to Beethoven's nephew Karl.

78. Always place the hands at the key-board so that the fingers can not be raised higher than is necessary; only in this way is it possible to produce a singing tone.

Reported by Schindler as Beethoven's view on pianoforte instruction. He hated a *staccato* style of playing and dubbed it "finger dancing" and "throwing the hands in the air."

ON HIS OWN WORKS

80. I haven't a single friend; I must live alone. But well I know that God is nearer to me than to the others of my art; I associate with Him without fear, I have always recognized and understood Him, and I have no fear for my music;—it can meet no evil fate. Those who understand it must become free from all the miseries that the others drag with them.

To Bettina von Arnim. (Bettina's letter to Goethe, May 28, 1810.)

81. The variations will prove a little difficult to play, particularly the trills in the coda; but let that not frighten you. It is so disposed that you need play only the trills, omitting the other notes because they are also in the violin part. I would never have written a thing of this kind had I not often noticed here and there in Vienna a man who after I had improvised of an evening would write down some of my peculiarities and make boast of them next day. Foreseeing that these things would soon appear in print I made up my mind to anticipate them. Another purpose which I had was to embarrass the local pianoforte masters. Many of them are my mortal enemies, and I wanted to have my revenge in this way, for I knew in advance that the varia-

tions would be put before them, and that they
would make exhibitions of themselves.

Vienna, November 2, 1793, to Eleonore von Breuning,
in dedicating to her the variations in F major, " Se vuol
ballare." (The pianist whom Beethoven accuses of steal-
ing his thunder was Abbé Gelinek.)

82. The time in which I wrote my sonatas
(the first ones of the second period) was more
poetical than the present (1823); such hints
were therefore unnecessary. Every one at that
time felt in the Largo of the third sonata in D
(op. 10) the pictured soul-state of a melancholy
being, with all the nuances of light and shade
which occur in a delineation of melancholy and
its phases, without requiring a key in the shape
of a superscription; and everybody then saw in
the two sonatas (op. 14) the picture of a con-
test between two principles, or a dialogue between two persons, because it was so obvious.

In answer to Schindler's question why he had not indicated the poetical conceits underlying his sonatas by
superscriptions or titles.

83. This sonata has a clean face (literally
" has washed itself "), my dear brother!

January, 1801, to Hofmeister, publisher in Leipsic, to
whom he offers the sonata, op. 22, for 20 ducats.

84. They are incessantly talking about the
C-sharp minor sonata (op. 27, No. 2); on my
word I have written better ones. The F-sharp
major sonata (op. 78) is a different thing!

A remark to Czerny. [The C-sharp minor sonata is
that popularly known as the " Moonlight Sonata," a title
which is wholly without warrant. Its origin is due to
Rellstab, who, in describing the first movement, drew a

picture of a small boat in the moonlight on Lake Lucerne. In Vienna a tradition that Beethoven had composed it in an arbor gave rise to the title " Arbor sonata." Titles of this character work much mischief in the amateur mind by giving rise to fantastic conceptions of the contents of the music. H. E. K.]

85. The thing which my brother can have from me is 1, a *Septett per il Violino, Viola, Violoncello, Contrabasso, Clarinetto, Corno, Fagotto, tutti obligati;* for I can not write anything that is not *obligato,* having come into the world with *obligato* accompaniment.

December 15, 1800, to Hofmeister, publisher, in Leipsic.

86. I am but little satisfied with my works thus far; from to-day I shall adopt a new course.

Reported by Carl Czerny in his autobiography in 1842. Concerning the time at which the remark was made, Czerny says: " It was said about 1803, when B. had composed op. 28 (the pianoforte sonata in D) to his friend Krumpholz (a violinist). Shortly afterward there appeared the sonatas (now op. 31) in which a partial fulfilment of his resolution may be observed."

87. Read Shakespeare's " Tempest."

An answer to Schindler's question as to what poetical conceit underlay the sonatas in F minor. Beethoven used playfully to call the little son of Breuning, the friend of his youth, *Ariel,* because he employed him often as a messenger. [" Schindler relates that when once he asked Beethoven to tell him what the F minor and D minor (op. 31, No. 2) meant, he received for an answer only the enigmatical remark: ' Read Shakespeare's " Tempest." ' Many a student and commentator has since read the ' Tempest ' in the hope of finding a clew to the emotional contents which Beethoven believed to be in the two works, so singularly associated, only to find himself baffled. It is a fancy, which rests, perhaps, too much on outward things, but still one full of suggestion, that had Bee-

thoven said: 'Hear my C minor symphony,' he would
have given a better starting-point to the imagination of
those who are seeking to know what the F minor sonata
means. Most obviously it means music, but it means
music that is an expression of one of those psychological
struggles which Beethoven felt called upon more and
more to delineate as he was more and more shut out from
the companionship of the external world. Such struggles
are in the truest sense of the word tempests. The motive,
which, according to the story, Beethoven himself said,
indicates, in the symphony, the rappings of Fate at the
door of human existence, is common to two works which
are also related in their spiritual contents. Singularly
enough, too, in both cases the struggle which is begun in
the first movement and continued in the third, is inter-
rupted by a period of calm, reassuring, soul-fortifying
aspiration, which, in the symphony as well as in the sonata, takes the form of a theme with variations." "How
to Listen to Music," page 29. H. E. K.]

**88. *Sinfonia Pastorella.* He who has ever
had a notion of country life can imagine for
himself without many superscriptions what the
composer is after. Even without a description
the whole, which is more sentiment than tone-
painting, will be recognized.**

A note among the sketches for the " Pastoral " symphony preserved in the Royal Library at Berlin. [There
are other notes of similar import among the sketches referred to which can profitably be introduced here. "The
hearer should be allowed to discover the situations;"
" *Sinfonia caracteristica,* or a recollection of country
life;" " Pastoral Symphony: No picture, but something in
which the emotions are expressed which are aroused in
men by the pleasure of the country (or) in which some
feelings of country life are set forth." When, finally,
the work was given to the publisher, Beethoven included
in the title an admonitory explanation which should have
everlasting validity: " Pastoral Symphony: more expression of feeling than painting." H. E. K.]

89. My "Fidelio" was not understood by the

public, but I know that it will yet be appreci-
ated; for though I am well aware of the value
of my " Fidelio " I know just as well that the
symphony is my real element. When sounds
ring in me I always hear the full orchestra; I
can ask anything of instrumentalists, but when
writing for the voice I must continually ask myself: " Can that be sung? "

A remark made in 1823 or 1824 to Griesinger.

90. Thus Fate knocks at the portals!

Reported by Schindler as Beethoven's explanation of
the opening of the symphony in C minor. [" Hofrath
Küffner told him (Krenn) that he once lived with Beethoven in Heiligenstadt, and that they were in the habit
evenings of going down to Nüssdorf to eat a fish supper
in the Gasthaus 'Zur Rose.' One evening when B. was
in a good humor, Küffner began: 'Tell me frankly which
is your favorite among your symphonies?' B. (in good
humor) 'Eh! Eh! The Eroica.' K. 'I should have
guessed the C minor.' B. 'No; the Eroica.' " From
Thayer's note-book. See " Music and Manners in the
Classical Period." H. E. K.]

91. The solo sonatas (op. 109-11?) are perhaps the best, but also the last, music that I
composed for the pianoforte. It is and always
will be an unsatisfactory instrument. I shall
hereafter follow the example of my grand-
master Händel, and every year write only an
oratorio and a concerto for some string or wind
instrument, provided I shall have finished my
tenth symphony (C minor) and Requiem.

Reported by Holz. As to the tenth symphony see note
to No. 95.

92. God knows why it is that my pianoforte

music always makes the worst impression on me, especially when it is played badly.

June 2, 1804. A note among the sketches for the "Leonore" overture.

93. Never did my own music produce such an effect upon me; even now when I recall this work it still costs me a tear.

Reported by Holz. The reference is to the Cavatina from the quartet in B-flat, op. 130, which Beethoven thought the crown of all quartet movements and his favorite composition. When alone and undisturbed he was fond of playing his favorite pianoforte Andante— that from the sonata op. 28.

94. I do not write what I most desire to, but that which I need to because of money. But this is not saying that I write only for money. When the present period is past, I hope at last to write that which is the highest thing for me as well as art,—" Faust."

From a conversation book used in 1823. To Bühler, tutor in the house of a merchant, who was seeking information about an oratorio which Beethoven had been commissioned to write by the Handel and Haydn Society of Boston.

95. Ha! " Faust; " that would be a piece of work! Something might come out of that! But for some time I have been big with three other large works. Much is already sketched out, that is, in my head. I must be rid of them first:—two large symphonies differing from each other, and each differing from all the others, and an oratorio. And this will take a long time. You see, for a considerable time I have had trouble to get myself to write. I sit and think,

and think I've long had the thing, but it will not on the paper. I dread the beginning of these large works. Once into the work, and it goes.

In the summer of 1822, to Rochlitz, at Baden. The symphonies referred to are the ninth and tenth. The latter existed only in Beethoven's mind and a few sketches. In it he intended to combine antique and modern views of life. " In the text Greek mythology, *cantique ecclésiastique;* in the Allegro, a Bacchic festival." Sketch-book of 1818. The oratorio was to have been called " The Victory of the Cross." It was not written. Schindler wrote to Moscheles in London about Beethoven in the last weeks of his life: " He said much about the plan of the tenth symphony. As the work had shaped itself in his imagination it might have become a musical monstrosity, compared with which his other symphonies would have been mere *opuscula*."

ON ART AND ARTISTS

96. How eagerly mankind withdraws from the poor artist what it has once given him;—and Zeus, from whom one might ask an invitation to sup on ambrosia, lives no longer.

In the summer of 1814, to Kauka, an advocate who represented him in the lawsuit against the heirs of Kinsky.

97. I love straightforwardness and uprightness, and believe that the artist ought not to be belittled; for, alas! brilliant as fame is externally, it is not always the privilege of the artist to be Jupiter's guest on Olympus all the time. Unfortunately vulgar humanity drags him down only too often and too rudely from the pure upper ether.

June 5, 1822, to C. F. Peters, music publisher, in Leipsic, when treating with him touching a complete edition of his works.

98. The true artist has no pride; unhappily he realizes that art has no limitations, he feels darkly how far he is from the goal, and while, perhaps he is admired by others, he grieves that he has not yet reached the point where the better genius shall shine before him like a distant sun.

Teplitz, July 17, to an admirer ten years old.

99. You yourself know what a change is

wrought by a few years in the case of an artist who is continually pushing forward. The greater the progress which one makes in art, the less is one satisfied with one's old works.

Vienna, August 4, 1800, to Mathisson, in the dedication of his setting of "Adelaide." "My most ardent wish will be fulfilled if you are not displeased with the musical composition of your heavenly 'Adelaide.'"

100. Those composers are exemplars who unite nature and art in their works.

Baden, in 1824, to Freudenberg, organist from Breslau.

101. What will be the judgment a century hence concerning the lauded works of our favorite composers to-day? Inasmuch as nearly everything is subject to the changes of time, and, more's the pity, the fashions of time, only that which is good and true, will endure like a rock, and no wanton hand will ever venture to defile it. Then let every man do that which is right, strive with all his might toward the goal which can never be attained, develop to the last breath the gifts with which a gracious Creator has endowed him, and never cease to learn; for "Life is short, art eternal!"

From the notes in the instruction book of Archduke Rudolph.

102. Famous artists always labor under an embarrassment;—therefore first works are the best, though they may have sprung out of dark ground.

Conversation-book of 1820.

103. A musician is also a poet; he also can feel himself transported by a pair of eyes into another and more beautiful world where greater souls make sport of him and set him right difficult tasks.

August 15, 1812, to Bettina von Arnim.

104. I told Goethe my opinion as to how applause affects men like us, and that we want our equals to hear us understandingly! Emotion suits women only; music ought to strike fire from the soul of a man.

August 15, 1812, to Bettina von Arnim.

105. Most people are touched by anything good; but they do not partake of the artist's nature; artists are ardent, they do not weep.

Reported to Goethe by Bettina von Arnim, May 28, 1810.

106. *L'art unit tout le monde,*—how much more the true artist!

March 15, 1823, to Cherubini, in Paris.

107. Only the artist, or the free scholar, carries his happiness within him.

Reported by Karl von Bursy as part of a conversation in 1816.

108. There ought to be only one large art warehouse in the world, to which the artist could carry his art-works and from which he could carry away whatever he needed. As it is one must be half a tradesman.

January, 1801, to Hofmeister, in Leipsic.

BEETHOVEN AS CRITIC

The opinion of artist on artists is a dubious
quantity. Recall the startling criticisms of
Böcklin on his associates in art made public by
the memoirs of his friends after his death. Such
judgments are often one-sided, not without
prejudice, and mostly the expression of impulse.
It is a different matter when the artist speaks
about the disciples of another art than his own,
even if the opinions which Böcklin and Wagner
held of each other are not a favorable example.
Where Beethoven speaks of other composers we
must read with clear and open eyes; but even
here there will be much with which we can be in
accord, especially his judgment on Rossini,
whom he hated so intensely, and whose airy,
sense-bewitching art seduced the Viennese from
Beethoven. Interesting and also characteristic
of the man is the attitude which he adopted
towards the poets of his time. In general he
estimated his contemporaries as highly as they
deserved.

109. Do not tear the laurel wreaths from the
heads of Händel, Haydn and Mozart; they belong to them,—not yet to me.

Teplitz, July 17, 1812, to his ten-year-old admirer,
Emilie M., who had given him a portfolio made by herself.

110. Pure church music ought to be performed by voices only, except a " Gloria," or
some similar text.   For this reason I prefer
Palestrina; but it is folly to imitate him without having his genius and religious views; it
would be difficult, if not impossible, too, for the
singers of to-day to sing his long notes in a
sustained and pure manner.

To Freudenberg, in 1824.

111. Händel is the unattained master of all
masters.   Go and learn from him how to achieve
vast effects with simple means.

Reported by Seyfried.   On his death-bed, about the
middle of February, 1827, he said to young Gerhard von
Breuning, on receiving Händel's works: " Händel is the
greatest and ablest of all composers; from him I can still
learn.   Bring me the books! "

112. Händel is the greatest composer that
ever lived.   I would uncover my head and kneel
on his grave.

Fall of 1823, to J. A. Stumpff, harp maker of London,
who acted very nobly toward Beethoven in his last days.
It was he who rejoiced the dying composer by sending
him the forty volumes of Händel's works (see 11).
[" Cipriani Potter, to A. W. T., February 27, 1861.   Beethoven used to walk across the fields to Vienna very
often.   B. would stop, look about and express his love
for nature.   One day Potter asked: ' Who is the greatest
living composer, yourself excepted? '   Beethoven seemed
puzzled for a moment, and then exclaimed: ' Cherubini! '
Potter went on: ' And of dead authors? '   B.—He had
always considered Mozart as such, but since he had been
made acquainted with Händel he put him at the head."
From A. W. Thayer's note-book, reprinted in " Music
and Manners in the Classical Period," page 208.   H.
E. K.]

113. Heaven forbid that I should take a journal in which sport is made of the *manes* of such a revered one.

Conversation-book of 1825, in reference to a criticism of Händel.

114. That you are going to publish Sebastian Bach's works is something which does good to my heart, which beats in love of the great and lofty art of this ancestral father of harmony; I want to see them soon.

January, 1801, to Hofmeister, in Leipsic.

115. Of Emanuel Bach's clavier works I have only a few, yet they must be not only a real delight to every true artist, but also serve him for study purposes; and it is for me a great pleasure to play works that I have never seen, or seldom see, for real art lovers.

July 26, 1809, to Gottfried Härtel, of Leipsic, in ordering all the scores of Haydn, Mozart and the two Bachs.

116. See, my dear Hummel, the birthplace of Haydn. I received it as a gift to-day, and it gives me great pleasure. A mean peasant hut, in which so great a man was born!

Remarked on his death-bed to his friend Hummel.

117. I have always reckoned myself among the greatest admirers of Mozart, and shall do so till the day of my death.

February 6, 1826, to Abbé Maximilian Stadler, who had sent him his essay on Mozart's "Requiem."

118. Cramer, Cramer! We shall never be able to compose anything like that!

To Cramer, after the two had heard Mozart's concerto in C-minor at a concert in the Augarten.

119. " Die Zauberflöte " will always remain Mozart's greatest work, for in it he for the first time showed himself to be a German musician. " Don Juan " still has the complete Italian cut; besides our sacred art ought never permit itself to be degraded to the level of a foil for so scandalous a subject.

A remark reported by Seyfried. [" Hozalka says that in 1820-21, as near as he can recollect, the wife of a Major Baumgarten took boy boarders in the house then standing where the Musikverein's Saal now is, and that Beethoven's nephew was placed with her. Her sister, Baronin Born, lived with her. One evening Hozalka, then a young man, called there and found only Baronin Born at home. Soon another caller came and stayed to tea. It was Beethoven. Among other topics Mozart came on the tapis, and the Born asked Beethoven (in writing, of course) which of Mozart's operas he thought most of. 'Die Zauberflöte,' said Beethoven, and, suddenly clasping his hands and throwing up his eyes, exclaimed: 'Oh, Mozart!' " From A. W. Thayer's notebooks, reprinted in " Music and Manners in the Classical Period," page 198. H. E. K.]

120. Say all conceivable pretty things to Cherubini,—that there is nothing I so ardently desire as that we should soon get another opera from him, and that of all our contemporaries I have the highest regard for him.

May 6, 1823, to Louis Schlösser, afterward chapelmaster in Darmstadt, who was about to undertake a journey to Paris. See note to No. 112.

121. Among all the composers alive Cherubini is the most worthy of respect. I am in complete agreement, too, with his conception of the "Requiem," and if ever I come to write one I shall take note of many things.

Remark reported by Seyfried. See No. 112.

122. Whoever studies Clementi thoroughly has simultaneously also learned Mozart and other authors; inversely, however, this is not the case.

Reported by Schindler.

123. There is much good in Spontini; he understands theatrical effect and martial noises admirably.

Spohr is so rich in dissonances; pleasure in his music is marred by his chromatic melody.

His name ought not to be Bach (brook), but Ocean, because of his infinite and inexhaustible wealth of tonal combinations and harmonies. Bach is the ideal of an organist.

In Baden, 1824, to Freudenberg.

124. The little man, otherwise so gentle,—I never would have credited him with such a thing. Now Weber must write operas in earnest, one after the other, without caring too much for refinement! *Kaspar*, the monster, looms up like a house; wherever the devil sticks in his claw we feel it.

To Rochlitz, at Baden, in the summer of 1822.

125. There you are, you rascal; you're a

devil of a fellow, God bless you! . . . .
Weber, you always were a fine fellow.

Beethoven's hearty greeting to Karl Maria von Weber,
in October, 1823.

126. K. M. Weber began too learn too late;
art did not have a chance to develop naturally
in him, and his single and obvious striving is to
appear brilliant.

A remark reported by Seyfried.

127. " Euryanthe " is an accumulation of
diminished seventh chords—all little backdoors!

Remarked to Schindler about Weber's opera.

128. Truly, a divine spark dwells in Schubert!

Said to Schindler when the latter made him acquainted
with the " Songs of Ossian," " Die Junge Nonne," " Die
Bürgschaft," "Grenzen der Menschheit," and other songs
of Schubert's.

129. There is nothing in Meyerbeer; he
hasn't the courage to strike at the right time.

To Tomaschek, in October, 1814, in a conversation
about the " Battle of Victoria," at the performance of
which, in 1813, Meyerbeer had played the big drum.

130. Rossini is a talented and a melodious
composer; his music suits the frivolous and sen-
suous spirit of the times, and his productivity
is such that he needs only as many weeks as the
Germans do years to write an opera.

In 1824, at Baden, to Freudenberg.

131. This rascal Rossini, who is not respected
by a single master of his art!

Conversation-book, 1825.

132. Rossini would have become a great composer if his teacher had frequently applied some blows *ad posteriora*.

Reported by Schindler. Beethoven had been reading the score of " Il Barbiere de Seviglia."

133. The Bohemians are born musicians. The Italians ought to take them as models. What have they to show for their famous conservatories? Behold! their idol, Rossini! If Dame Fortune had not given him a pretty talent and amiable melodies by the bushel, what he learned at school would have brought him nothing but potatoes for his big belly.

In a conversation-book at Haslinger's music shop, where Beethoven frequently visited.

134. Goethe has killed Klopstock for me. You wonder? Now you laugh? Ah, because I have read Klopstock! I carried him about with me for years when I walked. What besides? Well, I didn't always understand him. He skips about so; and he always begins so far away, above or below; always *Maestoso!* D-flat major! Isn't it so? But he's great, nevertheless, and uplifts the soul. When I couldn't understand him I sort of guessed at him.

To Rochlitz, in 1822.

135. As for me I prefer to set Homer, Klopstock, Schiller, to music; if it is difficult to do, these immortal poets at least deserve it.

To the directorate of the " Gesellschaft der Musikfreunde " of Vienna, January, 1824, in negotiations for an oratorio, " The Victory of the Cross " [which he had been commissioned to write by the Handel and Haydn Society of Boston. H. E. K.].

136. Goethe and Schiller are my favorite poets, as also Ossian and Homer, the latter of whom, unfortunately, I can read only in translation.

August 8, 1809, to Breitkopf and Härtel.

137. Who can sufficiently thank a great poet, —the most valuable jewel of a nation!

February 10, 1811, to Bettina von Arnim. The reference was to Goethe.

138. When you write to Goethe about me search out all the words which can express my deepest reverence and admiration. I am myself about to write to him about " Egmont " for which I have composed the music, purely out of love for his poems which make me happy.

February 10, 1811, to Bettina von Arnim.

139. I would have gone to death, yes, ten times to death for Goethe. Then, when I was in the height of my enthusiasm, I thought out my " Egmont " music. Goethe,—he lives and wants us all to live with him. It is for that reason that he can be composed. Nobody is so easily composed as he. But I do not like to compose songs.

To Rochlitz, in 1822, when Beethoven recalled Goethe's amiability in Teplitz.

140. Goethe is too fond of the atmosphere of the court; fonder than becomes a poet. There is little room for sport over the absurdities of

the virtuosi, when poets, who ought to be looked
upon as the foremost teachers of the nation,
can forget everything else in the enjoyment of
court glitter.

Franzensbrunn, August 9, 1812, to Gottfried Härtel
of Leipsic.

141. When two persons like Goethe and I
meet these grand folk must be made to see what
our sort consider great.

August 15, 1812, in a description of how haughtily he,
and how humbly Goethe, had behaved in the presence of
the Imperial court.

142. Since that summer in Carlsbad I read
Goethe every day,—when I read at all.

Remarked to Rochlitz.

143. Goethe ought not to write more; he will
meet the fate of the singers. Nevertheless he
will remain the foremost poet of Germany.

Conversation-book, 1818.

144. Can you lend me the "Theory of Col-
ors" for a few weeks? It is an important work.
His last things are insipid.

Conversation-book, 1820.

145. After all the fellow writes for money
only.

Reported by Schindler as having been said by Beethoven when, on his death-bed, he angrily threw a book
of Walter Scott's aside.

146. He, too, then, is nothing better than an
ordinary man! Now he will trample on all human rights only to humor his ambition; he will

place himself above all others,—become a tyrant!

With these words, as testified to by Ries, an eye-witness, Beethoven tore the title-page from the score of his "Eroica" symphony (which bore a dedication to Bonaparte) when the news reached him that Napoleon had declared himself emperor.

147. I believe that so long as the Austrian has his brown beer and sausage he will not revolt.

To Simrock, publisher, in Bonn, August 2, 1794.

148. Why do you sell nothing but music? Why did you not long ago follow my well-meant advice? Do get wise, and find your *raison.* Instead of a hundred-weight of paper order genuine unwatered Regensburger, float this much-liked article of trade down the Danube, serve it in measures, half-measures and seidels at cheap prices, throw in at intervals sausages, rolls, radishes, butter and cheese, invite the hungry and thirsty with letters an ell long on a sign: "Musical Beer House," and you will have so many guests at all hours of the day that one will hold the door open for the other and your office will never be empty.

To Haslinger, the music publisher, when the latter had complained about the indifference of the Viennese to music.

ON EDUCATION

Beethoven's observations on this subject were called out by his experiences in securing an education for his nephew Karl, son of his like-named brother, a duty which devolved on him on the death of his brother in the winter of 1815. He loved his nephew almost to idolatry, and hoped that he would honor the name of Beethoven in the future. But there was a frivolous vein in Karl, inherited probably from his mother, who was on easy footing with morality both before and after her husband's death. She sought with all her might to rid her son of the guardianship of his uncle. Karl was sent to various educational institutions and to these Beethoven sent many letters containing advice and instructions. The nephew grew to be more and more a care, not wholly without fault of the master. His passionate nature led to many quarrels between the two, all of which were followed by periods of extravagant fondness. Karl neglected his studies, led a frivolous life, was fond of billiards and the coffee-houses which were then generally popular, and finally, in the summer of 1826, made an attempt at suicide in the Helenental near Baden, which caused his social ostracism. When he was found he cried out: " I went to the bad because my uncle wanted to better me." Beethoven succeeded in

persuading Baron von Stutterheim, commander
of an infantry regiment at Iglau, to accept him
as an aspirant for military office. In later life
he became a respected official and man.

To Beethoven himself was vouchsafed only an
ill regulated education. His dissolute father
treated him now harshly, now gently. His
mother, who died early, was a silent sufferer,
had thoroughly understood her son, and to her
his love was devotion itself. He labored un-
wearyingly at his own intellectual and moral
advancement until his death.

It seems difficult to reconcile his almost extravagant estimate of the greatest possible liberty in the development of man with his demands
for strict constraint to which he frequently
gives expression; but he had recognized that it
is necessary to grow out of restraint into liberty. His model as a sensitive and sympathetic
educator was his motherly friend, the wife of
Court Councillor von Breuning in Bonn, of
whom he once said: " She knew how to keep the
insects off the blossoms."

Beethoven's views on musical education are to
be found in the chapters "On Composition" and
" On Performing Music."

149. Like the State, each man must have his
own constitution.
Diary, 1815.

150. Recommend virtue to your children;
that alone can bring happiness; not wealth,—

I speak from experience. It was virtue alone that bore me up in my misery; to her and my art I owe that I did not end my life by self-murder.

October 6, 1802, to his brothers Karl and Johann (the so-called Heiligenstadt Will).

151. I know no more sacred duty than to rear and educate a child.

January 7, 1820, in a communication to the Court of Appeals in the suit touching the guardianship of his nephew Karl.

152. Nature's weaknesses are nature's endowments; reason, the guide, must seek to lead and lessen them.

Diary, 1817.

153. It is man's habit to hold his fellow man in esteem because he committed no greater errors.

May 6, 1811, to Breitkopf and Härtel, in a letter complaining of faulty printing in some of his compositions.

154. There is nothing more efficient in enforcing obedience upon others than the belief on their part that you are wiser than they. . . . Without tears fathers can not inculcate virtue in their children, or teachers learning and wisdom in their pupils; even the laws, by compelling tears from the citizens, compel them also to strive for justice.

Diary, 1815.

155. It is only becoming in a youth to combine his duties toward education and advancement with those which he owes to his benefactor and supporter; this I did toward my parents.

May 12, 1825, to his nephew Karl.

156. You can not honor the memory of your father better than to continue your studies with the greatest zeal, and strive to become an honest and excellent man.

To his nephew, 1816-18.

157. Let your conduct always be amiable; through art and science the best and noblest of men are bound together and your future vocation will not exclude you.

Baden, July 18, 1825, to his nephew, who had decided to become a merchant.

158. It is very true that a drop will hollow a stone; a thousand lovely impressions are obliterated when children are placed in wooden institutions while they might receive from their parents the most soulful impressions which would continue to exert their influence till the latest age.

Diary, spring of 1817. Beethoven was dissatisfied with Giannatasio's school in which he had placed his nephew. "Karl is a different child after he has been with me a few hours" (Diary). In 1826, after the attempt at suicide, Beethoven said to Breuning: "My Karl was in an institute; educational institutions furnish forth only hothouse plants."

159. Drops of water wear away a stone in time, not by force but by continual falling. Only through tireless industry are the sciences achieved so that one can truthfully say: no day without its line,—*nulla dies sine linea.*

1799, in a sketch for a theoretical handbook for Archduke Rudolph.

ON HIS OWN DISPOSITION AND CHARACTER

So open-hearted and straightforward a character as Beethoven could not have pictured himself with less reserve or greater truthfulness than he did during his life. Frankness toward himself, frankness toward others (though sometimes it went to the extreme of rudeness and illbreeding) was his motto. The joyous nature which was his as a lad, and which was not at all averse to a merry prank now and then, underwent a change when he began to lose his hearing. The dread of deafness and its consequences drove him nearly to despair, so that he sometimes contemplated suicide. Increasing hardness of hearing gradually made him reserved, morose and gloomy. With the progress of the malady his disposition and character underwent a decided change,—a fact which may be said to account for the contradictions in his conduct and utterances. It made him suspicious, distrustful; in his later years he imagined himself cheated and deceived in the most trifling matters by relatives, friends, publishers, servants.

Nevertheless Beethoven's whole soul was filled with a high idealism which penetrated through

the miseries of his daily life; it was full, too, of
a great love toward humanity in general and his
unworthy nephew in particular. Towards his
publishers he often appeared covetous and
grasping, seeking to rake and scrape together
all the money possible; but this was only for
the purpose of assuring the future of his
nephew. At the same time, in a merry moment,
he would load down his table with all that
kitchen and cellar could provide, for the refec-
tion of his friends. Thus he oscillated continuously between two extremes; but the power which
swung the pendulum was always the aural malady. He grew peevish and capricious towards
his best friends, rude, even brutal at times in
his treatment of them; only in the next moment
to overwhelm them most pathetically with atten-
tions. Till the end of his life he remained a
sufferer from his passionate disposition over
which he gradually obtained control until, at
the end, one could almost speak of a sunny clari-
fication of his nature.

He has heedlessly been accused of having led
a dissolute life, of having been an intemperate
drinker. There would be no necessity of con-
tradicting such a charge even if there were a
scintilla of evidence to support it; a drinker is
not necessarily a dishonorable man, least of all
a musician who drinks. But the fact of the
matter is that it is not true. If once Beethoven
wrote a merry note about merrymaking with
friends, let us rejoice that occasions did some-

times occur, though but rarely, when the heart
of the sufferer was temporarily gladdened.

He was a strict moralist, as is particularly
evidenced by the notes in his journal which have
not been made public. In many things which be-
fell him in his daily life he was as ingenuous as a
child. His personality, on the whole, presented
itself in such a manner as to invite the intellectual and social Philistine to call him a fool.

160. I shall print a request in all the news-
papers that henceforth all artists refrain from
painting my picture without my knowledge; I
never thought that my own face would bring
me embarrassment.

About 1803, to Christine Gerardi, because without his
knowledge a portrait of him had been made somewhere
—in a café, probably.

161. Pity that I do not understand the art of
war as well as I do the art of music; I should
yet conquer Napoleon!

To Krumpholz, the violinist, when he informed Beethoven of the victory of Napoleon at Jena.

162. If I were a general and knew as much
about strategy as I, a composer, know about
counterpoint, I'd give you fellows something
to do.

Called out behind the back of a French officer, his fist
doubled, on May 12, 1809, when the French had occupied
Vienna. Reported by a witness, W. Rust.

163. Camillus, if I am not mistaken, was the
name of the Roman who drove the wicked Gauls

from Rome. At such a cost I would also take the name if I could drive them wherever I found them to where they belong.

To Pleyel, publisher, in Paris, April, 1807.

164. I love most the realm of mind which, to me, is the highest of all spiritual and temporal monarchies.

To Advocate Kauka in the summer of 1814. He had been speaking about the monarchs represented in the Congress of Vienna.

165. I shall not come in person, since that would be a sort of farewell, and farewells I have always avoided.

January 24, 1818, to Giannatasio del Rio, on taking his nephew Karl out of the latter institute.

166. I hope still to bring a few large works into the world, and then, like an old child, to end my earthly career somewhere among good people.

October 6, 1802, to Wegeler.

167. O ye men, who think or declare me to be hostile, morose or misanthropical, what injustice ye do me! Ye know not the secret cause of what thus appears to you. My heart and mind were from childhood disposed for the tender feelings of benevolence; I was always wishing to accomplish great deeds.

October 6, 1802, in the so-called Heiligenstadt Will.

168. Divinity, thou lookest into my heart, thou knowest it, thou knowest that love for mankind and a desire to do good have their abode

there. O ye men, when one day ye read this think that ye have wronged me, and may the unfortunate console himself with the thought that he has found one of his kind who, despite all the obstacles which nature put in his path, yet did all in his power to be accepted in the ranks of worthy artists and men!

From the Heiligenstadt Will.

169. I spend all my mornings with the muses;—and they bless me also in my walks.

October 12, 1825, to his nephew Karl.

170. Concerning myself nothing,—that is, from nothing nothing.

October 19, 1815, to Countess Erdödy.

171. Beethoven can write, thank God; but do nothing else on earth.

December 22, 1822, to Ferdinand Ries, in London.

172. Mentally I often frame an answer, but when I come to write it down I generally throw the pen aside, since I am not able to write what I feel.

October 7, 1826, to his friend Wegeler, in Coblenz. "The better sort of people, I think, know me anyhow." He is excusing his laziness in letter-writing.

173. I have the gift to conceal my sensitiveness touching a multitude of things; but when I am provoked at a moment when I am more sensitive than usual to anger, I burst out more violently than anybody else.

July 24, 1804, to Ries, in reporting to him a quarrel with Stephan von Breuning.

174. X. is completely changed since I threw half a dozen books at her head. Perhaps something of their contents accidentally got into her head or her wicked heart.

To Mme. Streicher, who often had to put Beethoven's house in order.

175. I can have no intercourse, and do not want to have any, with persons who are not willing to believe in me because I have not yet made a wide reputation.

To Prince Lobkowitz, about 1798. A cavalier had failed to show him proper respect in the Prince's salon.

176. Many a vigorous and unconsidered word drops from my mouth, for which reason I am considered mad.

In the summer of 1820, to Dr. Müller, of Bremen, who was paying him a visit.

177. I will grapple with Fate; it shall not quite bear me down. O, it is lovely to live life a thousand times!

November 16, 1800, or 1801, to Wegeler.

178. Morality is the strength of men who distinguish themselves over others, and it is mine.

In a communication to his friend, Baron Zmeskall.

179. I, too, am a king!

Said to Holz, when the latter begged him not to sell the ring which King Frederick William III, of Prussia, had sent to him instead of money or an order in return for the dedication of the ninth symphony. "Master, keep the ring," Holz had said, "it is from a king." Beethoven made his remark "with indescribable dignity and self-consciousness." On his death-bed he said to lit-

tle Gerhard von Breuning: "Know that I am an artist."
At the height of the popular infatuation for Rossini
(1822) he said to his friends: "Well, they will not be
able to rob me of my place in the history of art."

180. Prince, what you are you are by accident of birth; what I am, I am through my own efforts. There have been thousands of princes and will be thousands more; there is only one Beethoven!

According to tradition, from a letter which he wrote
to Prince Lichnowsky when the latter attempted to per-
suade him to play for some French officers on his estate
in Silesia. Beethoven went at night to Troppau, carrying the manuscript of the (so-called) "Appassionata"
sonata, which suffered from the rain.

181. My nobility is here, and here (pointing to his heart and head).

Reported by Schindler. In the lawsuit against his
sister-in-law (the mother of nephew Karl) Beethoven
had been called on to prove that the "van" in his name
was a badge of nobility.

182. You write that somebody has said that I am the natural son of the late King of Prussia. The same thing was said to me long ago, but I have made it a rule never to write anything about myself or answer anything that is said about me.

October 7, 1826, to Wegeler. "I leave it to you to
give the world an account of myself and especially my
mother." The statement had appeared in Brockhaus's
"Lexicon."

183. To me the highest thing, after God, is my honor.

July 26, 1822, to the publisher Peters, in Leipsic.

184. I have never thought of writing for reputation and honor. What I have in my heart must out; that is the reason why I compose.

Remark to Karl Czerny, reported in his autobiography.

185. I do not desire that you shall esteem me greater as an artist, but better and more perfect as a man; when the condition of our country is somewhat better, then my art shall be devoted to the welfare of the poor.

Vienna, June 29, 1800, to Wegeler, in Bonn, writing of his return to his native land.

186. Perhaps the only thing that looks like genius about me is that my affairs are not always in the best of order, and that in this respect nobody can be of help but myself.

April 22, 1801, to Hofmeister, in Leipsic, excusing himself for dilatoriness in sending him compositions (Pianoforte sonata op. 22, symphony op. 21, septet op. 20 and concerto op. 19).

187. I am free from all small vanities. Only in the divine art is the lever which gives me power to sacrifice the best part of my life to the celestial muses.

September 9, 1824, to George Nägeli, in Zurich.

188. Inasmuch as the purpose of the undersigned throughout his career has not been selfish but the promotion of the interests of art, the elevation of popular taste and the flight of his own genius toward loftier ideals and perfection, it was inevitable that he should fre-

quently sacrifice his own advantages and profit
to the muse.

December, 1804, to the Director of the Court Theatre,
applying for an engagement which was never effected.

189. From my earliest childhood my zeal to
serve suffering humanity with my art was never
content with any kind of a subterfuge; and no
other reward is needed than the internal satis-
faction which always accompanies such a deed.

To Procurator Varenna, who had asked him for compositions to be played at a charity concert in Graz.

190. There is no greater pleasure for me
than to practise and exhibit my art.

November 16, 1800, or 1801, to Wegeler.

191. I recognize no other accomplishments or
advantages than those which place one amongst
the better class of men; where I find them, there
is my home.

Teplitz, July 17, 1812, to his little admirer, Emile M.,
in H.

192. From childhood I learned to love virtue,
and everything beautiful and good.

About 1808, to Frau Marie Bigot.

193. It is one of my foremost principles
never to occupy any other relations than those
of friendship with the wife of another man. I
should never want to fill my heart with distrust
towards those who may chance some day to
share my fate with me, and thus destroy the
loveliest and purest life for myself.

About 1808, to Frau Marie Bigot, after she had de-
clined his invitation to drive with him.

194. In my solitude here I miss my room-mate, at least at evening and noon, when the human animal is obliged to assimilate that which is necessary to the production of the intellectual, and which I prefer to do in company with another.

Teplitz, September 6, 1811, to Tiedge.

195. It was not intentional and premeditated malice which led me to act toward you as I did; it was my unpardonable carelessness.

To Wegeler.

196. I am not bad; hot blood is my wickedness, my crime is youthfulness. I am not bad, really not bad; even though wild surges often accuse my heart, it still is good. To do good wherever we can, to love liberty above all things, and never to deny truth though it be at the throne itself.—Think occasionally of the friend who honors you.

Written in the autograph album of a Herr Bocke.

197. It is a singular sensation to see and hear one's self praised, and then to be conscious of one's own imperfections as I am. I always regard such occasions as admonitions to get nearer the unattainable goal set for us by art and nature, hard as it may be.

To Mdlle. de Girardi, who had sung his praises in a poem.

198. It is my sincere desire that whatever shall be said of me hereafter shall adhere

strictly to the truth in every respect regardless of who may be hurt thereby, me not excepted.

Reported by Schindler, who also relates that when Beethoven handed him documents to be used in the biography a week before his death, he said to him and Breuning: "But in all things severely the truth; for that I hold you to a strict accountability."

199. Now you can help me to find a wife. If you find a beautiful woman in F. who, mayhap, endows my music with a sigh,—but she must be no Elise Bürger—make a provisional engagement. But she must be beautiful, for I can love only the beautiful; otherwise I might love myself.

In 1809, to Baron von Gleichenstein. As for the personal reference it seems likely that Beethoven referred to Elise Bürger, second wife of the poet G. August Bürger, with whom he had got acquainted after she had been divorced and become an elocutionist.

200. Am I not a true friend? Why do you conceal your necessities from me? No friend of mine must suffer so long as I have anything.

To Ferdinand Ries, in 1801. Ries's father had been kind to Beethoven on the death of his mother in 1787.

201. I would rather forget what I owe to myself than what I owe to others.

To Frau Streicher, in the summer of 1817.

202. I never practise revenge. When I must antagonize others I do no more than is necessary to protect myself against them, or prevent them from doing further evil.

To Frau Streicher, in reference to the troubles which his servants gave him, many of which, no doubt, were due to faults of his own, excusable in a man in his condition of health.

203. Be convinced that mankind, even in your case, will always be sacred to me.

To Czapka, Magisterial Councillor, August, 1826, in the matter of his nephew's attempt at suicide.

204. H. is, and always will be, too weak for friendship, and I look upon him and Y. as mere instruments upon which I play when I feel like it; but they can never be witnesses of my internal and external activities, and just as little real participants. I value them according as they do me service.

Summer of 1800, to the friend of his youth, Pastor Amenda. H. was probably the faithful Baron Zmeskall von Domanowectz.

205. If it amuses them to talk and write about me in that manner, let them go on.

Reported by Schindler as referring to critics who had declared him ripe for the madhouse.

206. To your gentlemen critics I recommend a little more foresight and shrewdness, particularly in respect of the products of younger authors, as many a one, who might otherwise make progress, may be frightened off. So far as I am concerned I am far from thinking myself so perfect as not to be able to endure faulting; yet at the beginning the clamor of your critic was so debasing that I could scarcely discuss the matter when I compared myself with others, but had to remain quiet and think: they do not understand. I was the more able to remain quiet when I recalled how men were praised who signify little among those who know, and who have almost disappeared despite their good points. Well, *pax vobiscum*, peace to them and me,—I would never have mentioned a syllable had you not begun.

April 22, 1801, to Breitkopf and Härtel, publishers of the " Allgemeine Musik Zeitung."

207. Who was happier than I when I could still pronounce the sweet word " mother " and have it heard? To whom can I speak it now?

September 15, 1787, from Bonn to Dr. Schade, of Augsburg, who had aided him in his return journey from Vienna to Bonn. His mother had died on July 17, 1787.

208. I seldom go anywhere since it was always impossible for me to associate with people where there was not a certain exchange of ideas.

February 15, 1817, to Brentano of Frankfort.

209. Not a word about rest! I know of none except in sleep, and sorry enough am I that I am obliged to yield up more to it than formerly.

November 16, 1801, or 1802, to Wegeler. In Homer's " Odyssey " Beethoven thickly underscored the words: " Too much sleep is injurious." XV, 393.

210. Rest assured that you are dealing with a true artist who likes to be paid decently, it is true, but who loves his own reputation and also the fame of his art; who is never satisfied with himself and who strives continually to make even greater progress in his art.

November 23, 1809, to George Thomson, of Edinburgh, for whom Beethoven arranged the Scotch songs.

211. My motto is always: *nulla dies sine linea;* and if I permit the muse to go to sleep it is only that she may awake strengthened.

October 7, 1826, to Wegeler.

212. There is no treatise likely to be too learned for me. Without laying claim to real learning it is yet true that since my childhood I have striven to learn the minds of the best and wisest of every period of time. It is a disgrace for every artist who does not try to do as much.

November 2, 1809, to Breitkopf and Härtel, of Leipsic.

213. Without wishing in the least to set myself up as an exemplar I assure you that I lived in a small and insignificant place, and made out of myself nearly all that I was there and am here;—this to your comfort in case you feel the need of making progress in art.

Baden, July 6, 1804, to Herr Wiedebein, of Brunswick, who had asked if it was advisable for a music teacher and student to make his home in Vienna.

214. There is much on earth to be done,—do it soon! I must not continue my present everyday life,—art asks this sacrifice also. Take rest in diversion in order to work more energetically.

Diary, 1814.

215. The daily grind exhausts me.

Baden, August 23, 1823, to his nephew Karl.

THE SUFFERER

216. Compelled to be a philosopher as early as my 28th year;—it is not an easy matter,—more difficult for the artist than any other man.

October 6, 1802; the Heiligenstadt Will.

217. Compelled to contemplate a lasting malady, born with an ardent and lively temperament, susceptible to the diversions of society, I was obliged at an early date to isolate myself and live a life of solitude.

From the same.

218. It was impossible for me to say to others: speak louder; shout! for I am deaf. Ah! was it possible for me to proclaim a deficiency in that one sense which in my case ought to have been more perfect than in all others, which I had once possessed in greatest perfection, to a degree of perfection, indeed, which few of my profession have ever enjoyed?

From the same.

219. For me there can be no recreation in human society, refined conversation, mutual exchange of thoughts and feelings; only so far as necessity compels may I give myself to society,—I must live like an exile.

From the same.

220. How great was the humiliation when

one who stood beside me heard the distant sound
of a shepherd's pipe, and I heard nothing; or
heard the shepherd singing, and I heard nothing. Such experiences brought me to the verge
of despair;—but little more and I should have
put an end to my life. Art, art alone deterred
me.

From the same.

221. I may say that I live a wretched existence. For almost two years I have avoided all
social gatherings because it is impossible for me
to tell the people I am deaf. If my vocation
were anything else it might be more endurable,
but under the circumstances the condition is ter-
rible; besides what would my enemies say,—they
are not few in number! To give you an idea
of this singular deafness let me tell you that in
the theatre I must lean over close to the orchestra in order to understand the actor; if I am a
little remote from them I do not hear the high
tones of instruments and voices; it is remarkable
that there are persons who have not observed it,
but because I am generally absent-minded my
conduct is ascribed to that.

Vienna, June 29, 1800, to Wegeler. "To you only do
I confide this as a secret." Concerning his deafness see
Appendix.

222. My defective hearing appeared every-
where before me like a ghost; I fled from the
presence of men, was obliged to appear to be a
misanthrope although I am so little such.

November 16, 1801, or 1800, to Wegeler, in writing to

him about his happy love. " Unfortunately, she is not of my station in life."

223. Truly, a hard lot has befallen me! Yet I accept the decree of Fate, and continually pray to God to grant that as long as I must endure this death in life, I may be preserved from want.

March 14, 1827, to Moscheles, after Beethoven had undergone the fourth operation for dropsy and was confronting the fifth. He died on March 26, 1827.

224. Live alone in your art! Restricted though you be by your defective sense, this is still the only existence for you.

Diary, 1816.

225. Dissatisfied with many things, more susceptible than any other person and tormented by my deafness, I often find only suffering in the association with others.

In 1815, to Brauchle, tutor in the house of Countess Erdödy.

226. I have emptied a cup of bitter suffering and already won martyrdom in art through the kindness of art's disciples and my art associates.

In the summer of 1814, to Advocate Kauka. "Socrates and Jesus were my exemplars," he remarks in a Conversation-book of 1819.

227. Perfect the ear trumpets as far as possible, and then travel; this you owe to yourself, to mankind and to the Almighty! Only thus can you develop all that is still locked within you;—and a little court,—a little chapel,—I

writing the music and having it performed to
the glory of the Almighty, the Eternal, the Infinite——!

Diary, 1815. Beethoven was hoping to receive an ap-
pointment as chapelmaster from his former pupil, Archduke Rudolph, Archbishop of Olmütz.

228. God help me! Thou seest me deserted
by all mankind. I do not want to do wrong,—
hear my prayer to be with my Karl in the future for which there seems to be no possibility
now. O, harsh Fate, cruel destiny. No, my unhappy condition will never end. "This I feel
and recognize clearly: Life is not the greatest
of blessings; but the greatest of evils is guilt."
(From Schiller's "Braut von Messina"). There
is no salvation for you except to hasten away
from here; only by this means can you lift yourself again to the heights of your art whereas
you are here sinking to the commonplace,—
and a symphony—and then away,—away,—
meanwhile fund the salaries which can be done
for years. Work during the summer preparatory to travel; only thus can you do the great
work for your poor nephew; later travel through
Italy, Sicily, with a few other artists.

Diary, spring of 1817. The salaries were the annuities
paid him for several years by Archduke Rudolph, Prince
Kinsky and Prince Lobkowitz. Seume's "Spaziergang
nach Syrakus" was a favorite book of Beethoven's and
inspired him in a desire to make a similar tour, but nothing came of it.

229. You must not be a man like other men;
not for yourself, only for others; for you there

is no more happiness except in yourself, in your art.—O God, give me strength to overcome myself, nothing must hold me to this life.

Beginning of the Diary, 1812-18.

230. Leave operas and all else alone, write only for your orphan, and then a cowl to close this unhappy life.

Diary, 1816.

231. I have often cursed my existence; Plutarch taught me resignation. I shall, if possible, defy Fate, though there will be hours in my life when I shall be the most miserable of God's creatures. Resignation! What a wretched resort; yet it is the only one left me!

Vienna, June 29, 1800, to Wegeler.

232. Patience, they tell me, I must now choose for a guide. I have done so. It shall be my resolve, lastingly, I hope, to endure until it pleases the implacable Parcæ to break the thread. There may be improvement,—perhaps not,—I am prepared.

From the Heiligenstadt Will.

233. Let all that is called life be offered to the sublime and become a sanctuary of art. Let me live, even through artificial means, so they can be found.

Diary, 1814, when Beethoven was being celebrated extraordinarily by the royalties and dignitaries gathered at the Congress of Vienna.

234. Ah! it seemed impossible for me to leave the world until I had produced all that I felt

called upon to produce; and so I prolonged this wretched existence.

From the Heiligenstadt Will.

235. With joy shall I hasten forward to meet death; if he comes before I shall have had an opportunity to develop all my artistic capabilities, he will come too early in spite of my harsh fate, and I shall probably wish him to come at a later date. But even then I shall be content, for will he not release me from endless suffering? Come when you please, I shall meet you bravely.

From the Heiligenstadt Will.

236. Apollo and the muses will not yet permit me to be delivered over to the grim skeleton, for I owe them so much, and I must, on my departure for the Elysian Fields, leave behind me all that the spirit has inspired and commanded to be finished.

September 17, 1824, to Schott, music publisher in Mayence.

237. Had I not read somewhere that it is not permitted man to part voluntarily from his life so long as there is a good deed which he can perform, I should long since have been no more, —and by my own hand. O, how beautiful life is, but in my case it is poisoned.

May 2, 1810, to his friend Wegeler, to whom he is lamenting over " the demon that has set up his habitation in my ears."

238. I must abandon wholly the fond hope, which I brought hither, to be cured at least in a degree. As the fallen autumn leaves have

withered, so are now my hopes blighted. I depart in almost the same condition in which I came; even the lofty courage which often animated me in the beautiful days of summer has disappeared.

From the Will. Beethoven had tried the cure at Heiligenstadt.

239. All week long I had to suffer and endure like a saint. Away with this rabble! What a reproach to our civilization that we need what we despise and must always know it near!

In 1825, complaining of the misery caused by his domestics.

240. The best thing to do not to think of your malady is to keep occupied.

Diary, 1812-18.

241. It is no comfort for men of the better sort to say to them that others also suffer; but, alas! comparisons must always be made, though they only teach that we all suffer, that is err, only in different ways.

In 1816, to Countess Erdödy, on the death of her son.

242. The portraits of Händel, Bach, Gluck, Mozart and Haydn in my room,—they may help me to make claim on toleration.

Diary, 1815-16.

243. God, who knows my innermost soul, and knows how sacredly I have fulfilled all the duties put upon me as man by humanity, God and nature will surely some day relieve me from these afflictions.

July 18, 1821, to Archduke Rudolph, from Unter-Döbling.

244. Friendship and similar sentiments bring only wounds to me. Well, so be it; for you, poor Beethoven, there is no outward happiness; you must create it within you,—only in the world of ideality shall you find friends.

About 1808, to Baron von Gleichenstein, by whom he thought himself slighted.

245. You are living on a quiet sea, or already in the safe harbor; you do not feel the distress of a friend out in the raging storm,— or you must not feel it.

In 1811, to his friend Gleichenstein, when Beethoven was in love with the Baron's sister-in-law, Therese Malfatti.

246. I must have a confidant at my side lest life become a burden.

July 4, 1812, to Count Brunswick, whom he is urging to make a tour with him, probably to Teplitz.

247. Your love makes me at once the happiest and the unhappiest of men. At my age I need a certain uniformity and equableness of life; can such exist in our relationship?

June 7, 1800 (?), to the "Immortal Beloved."

248. O Providence! vouchsafe me one day of pure joy! Long has the echo of perfect felicity been absent from my heart. When O, when, O Thou Divine One, shall I feel it again in nature's temple and man's? Never? Ah! that would be too hard!

Conclusion of the Heiligenstadt Will.

WORLDLY WISDOM

249. Freedom,—progress, is purpose in the art-world as in universal creation, and if we moderns have not the hardihood of our ancestors, refinement of manners has surely accomplished something.

Mödling, July 29, 1819, to Archduke Rudolph.

250. The boundaries are not yet fixed which shall call out to talent and industry: thus far and no further!

Reported by Schindler.

251. You know that the sensitive spirit must not be bound to miserable necessities.

In the summer of 1814, to Johann Kauka, the advocate who represented him in the prosecution of his claims against the heirs of Prince Kinsky.

252. Art, the persecuted one, always finds an asylum. Did not Dædalus, shut up in the labyrinth, invent the wings which carried him out into the open air? O, I shall find them, too, these wings!

February 19, 1812, to Zmeskall, when, in 1811, by decree of the Treasury, the value of the Austrian currency was depreciated one-fifth, and the annuity which Beethoven received from Archduke Rudolph and the Princes Lobkowitz and Kinsky reduced to 800 florins.

253. Show me the course where at the goal there stands the palm of victory! Lend sublim-

ity to my loftiest thoughts, bring to them truths
that shall live forever!

Diary, 1814, while working on " Fidelio."

254. Every day is lost in which we do not
learn something useful. Man has no nobler or
more valuable possession than time; therefore
never put off till to-morrow what you can do
to-day.

From the notes in Archduke Rudolph's instruction-
book.

255. This is the mark of distinction of a
truly admirable man: steadfastness in times of
trouble.

Diary, 1816.

256. Courage, so it be righteous, will gain
all things.

April, 1815, to Countess Erdödy.

257. Force, which is a unit, will always pre-
vail against the majority which is divided.

Conversation-book, 1819.

258. Kings and Princes can create profes-
sors and councillors, and confer orders and
decorations; but they can not create great men,
spirits that rise above the earthly rabble;
these they can not create, and therefore they
are to be respected.

August 15, 1812, to Bettina von Arnim.

259. Man, help yourself!

Written under the words: "*Fine*, with the help of
God," which Moscheles had written at the end of a pianoforte arrangement of a portion of " Fidelio."

260. If I could give as definite expression to my thoughts about my illness as to my thoughts in music, I would soon help myself.

September, 1812, to Amalie Sebald, a patient at the cure in Teplitz.

261. Follow the advice of others only in the rarest cases.

Diary, 1816.

262. " The moral law in us, and the starry sky above us."—Kant.

Conversation-book, February, 1820. Literally the passage reads as follows in Kant's " Critique of Practical Reason: " " Two things fill the soul with ever new and increasing wonder and reverence the oftener the mind dwells upon them:—the starry sky above me and the moral law in me."

263. Blessed is he who has overcome all passions and then proceeds energetically to perform his duties under all circumstances careless of success! Let the motive lie in the deed, not in the outcome. Be not one of those whose spring of action is the hope of reward. Do not let your life pass in inactivity. Be industrious, do your duty, banish all thoughts as to the results, be they good or evil; for such equanimity is attention to intellectual things. Seek an asylum only in Wisdom; for he who is wretched and unhappy is so only in consequence of things. The truly wise man does not concern himself with the good and evil of this world. Therefore endeavor diligently to preserve this use of

your reason; for in the affairs of this world such a use is a precious art.

Diary. Though essentially in the language of Beethoven there is evidence that the passage was inspired by something that he had read.

264. The just man must be able also to suffer injustice without deviating in the least from the right course.

To the Viennese magistrate in the matter of Karl's education.

265. Man's humility towards man pains me; and yet when I consider myself in connection with the universe, what am I and what is he whom we call the greatest? And yet herein, again, lies the divine element in man.

To the "Immortal Beloved," July 6 (1800?).

266. Only the praise of one who has enjoyed praise can give pleasure.

Conversation-book, 1825.

267. Nothing is more intolerable than to be compelled to accuse one's self of one's own errors.

Teplitz, September 6, 1811, to Tiedge. Beethoven regrets that through his own fault he had not made Tiedge's acquaintance on an earlier opportunity.

268. What greater gift can man receive than fame, praise and immortality?

Diary, 1816-17. After Pliny, Epist. III.

269. Frequently it seems as if I should almost go mad over my undeserved fame; fortune seeks

me out and I almost fear new misfortune on that account.

July, 1810, to his friend Zmeskall. "Every day there come new inquiries from strangers, new acquaintances, new relationships."

270. The world must give one recognition,— it is not always unjust. I care nothing for it because I have a higher goal.

August 15, 1812, to Bettina von Arnim.

271. I have the more turned my gaze upwards; but for our own sakes and for others we are obliged to turn our attention sometimes to lower things; this, too, is a part of human destiny.

February 8, 1823, to Zelter, with whom he is negotiating the sale of a copy of the Mass in D.

272. Why so many dishes? Man is certainly very little higher than the other animals if his chief delights are those of the table.

Reported by J. A. Stumpff, in the "Harmonicon" of 1824. He dined with Beethoven in Baden.

273. Whoever tells a lie is not pure of heart, and such a person can not cook a clean soup.

To Mme. Streicher, in 1817, or '18, after having dismissed an otherwise good housekeeper because she had told a falsehood to spare his feelings.

274. Vice walks through paths full of present lusts and persuades many to follow it. Virtue pursues a steep path and is less seductive to mankind, especially if at another place there are persons who call them to a gently declining road.

Diary, 1815.

275. Sensual enjoyment without a union of souls is bestial and will always remain bestial; after it one experiences not a trace of noble sentiment, but rather regret.

Diary, 1812-18.

276. Men are not only together when they are with each other; even the distant and the dead live with us.

To Therese Malfatti, later Baroness von Drossdick, to whom in the country he sent Goethe's "Wilhelm Meister" and Schlegel's translation of Shakespeare.

277. There is no goodness except the possession of a good soul,—which may be seen in all things, from which one need not seek to hide.

August 15, 1812, to Bettina von Arnim.

278. The foundation of friendship demands the greatest likeness of human souls and hearts.

Baden, July 24, 1804, to Ries, describing his quarrel with Breuning.

279. True friendship can rest only on the union of like natures.

Diary, 1812-18.

280. The people say nothing; they are merely people. As a rule they only see themselves in others, and what they see is nothing; away with them! The good and the beautiful needs no people,—it exists without outward help, and this seems to be the reason of our enduring friendship.

September 16, 1812, to Amalie Sebald, in Teplitz, who had playfully called him a tyrant.

281. Look, my dear Ries; these are the great connoisseurs who affect to be able to judge of any piece of music so correctly and keenly. Give them but the name of their favorite,—they need no more!

To his pupil Ries, who had, as a joke, played a mediocre march at a gathering at Count Browne's and announced it to be a composition by Beethoven. When the march was praised beyond measure Beethoven broke out into a grim laugh.

282. Do not let all men see the contempt which they deserve; we do not know when we may need them.

Note in the Diary of 1814, after having had an unpleasant experience with his "friend" Bertolini. "Henceforth never step inside his house; shame on you to ask anything from such an one."

283. Our Time stands in need of powerful minds who will scourge these petty, malicious and miserable scoundrels,—much as my heart resents doing injury to a fellow man.

In 1825, to his nephew, in reference to the publication of a satirical canon on the Viennese publisher, Haslinger, by Schott, of Mayence.

284. To-day is Sunday. Shall I read something for you from the Gospels? "Love ye one another!"

To Frau Streicher.

285. Hate reacts on those who nourish it.

Diary, 1812-18.

286. When friends get into a quarrel it is

always best not to call in an intermediary, but to have friend turn to friend direct.

Vienna, November 2, 1793, to Eleonore von Breuning, of Bonn.

287. There are reasons for the conduct of men which one is not always willing to explain, but which, nevertheless, are based on ineradicable necessity.

In 1815, to Brauchle.

288. I was formerly inconsiderate and hasty in the expression of my opinions, and thereby I made enemies. Now I pass judgment on no one, and, indeed, for the reason that I do not wish to do any one harm. Moreover, in the last instance I always think: if it is something decent it will maintain itself in spite of all attack and envy; if there is nothing good and sound at the bottom of it, it will fall to pieces of itself, bolster it up as one may.

In a conversation with Tomaschek, in October, 1814.

289. Even the most sacred friendship may harbor secrets, but you ought not to misinterpret the secret of a friend because you can not guess it.

About 1808, to Frau Marie Bigot.

290. You are happy; it is my wish that you remain so, for every man is best placed in his sphere.

Baden, July 13, 1825, to his brother Johann, landowner in Gneixendorf.

291. One must not measure the cost of the useful.

To his nephew Karl in a discussion touching the purchase of an expensive book.

292. It is not my custom to prattle away my purposes, since every intention once betrayed is no longer one's own.

To Frau Streicher.

293. How stupidity and wretchedness always go in pairs!

Diary, 1817. Beethoven was greatly vexed by his servants.

294. Hope nourishes me; it nourishes half the world, and has been my neighbor all my life, —else what had become of me!

August 11, 1810, to Bettina von Arnim.

295. Fortune is round like a globe, hence, naturally, does not always fall on the noblest and best.

Vienna, July 29, 1800, to Wegeler.

296. Show your power, Fate! We are not our own masters; what is decided must be,—and so be it!

Diary, 1812-18.

297. Eternal Providence omnisciently directs the good and evil fortunes of mortal men.

Diary, 1818.

298. With tranquility, O God, will I submit myself to changes, and place all my trust in Thy unalterable mercy and goodness.

Diary, 1818.

299. All misfortune is mysterious and greatest when viewed alone; discussed with others it seems more endurable because one becomes entirely familiar with the things one dreads, and feels as if one had overcome it.

Diary, 1816.

300. One must not flee for protection to poverty against the loss of riches, nor to a lack of friendship against the loss of friends, nor by abstention from procreation against the death of children, but to reason against everything.

Diary, 1816.

301. I share deeply with you the righteous sorrow over the death of your wife. It seems to me that such a parting, which confronts nearly every married man, ought to keep one in the ranks of the unmarried.

May 20, 1811, to Gottfried Härtel, of Leipsic.

302. He who is afflicted with a malady which he can not alter, but which gradually brings him nearer and nearer to death, without which he would have lived longer, ought to reflect that murder or another cause might have killed him even more quickly.

Diary, 1812-18.

303. We finite ones with infinite souls are born only for sorrows and joy and it might almost be said that the best of us receive joy through sorrow.

October 19, 1815, to Countess Erdödy.

304. He is a base man who does not know how to die; I knew it as a boy of fifteen.

In the spring of 1816, to Miss Fanny Giannatasio del Rio, when Beethoven felt ill and spoke of dying. It is not known that he was ever near death in his youth.

305. A second and third generation recompenses me three and fourfold for the ill-will which I had to endure from by former contemporaries.

Copied into his Diary from Goethe's "Westöstlichen Divan."

306. " My hour at last is come;
    Yet not ingloriously or passively
    I die, but first will do some valiant deed,
    Of which mankind shall hear in after
        time."—Homer.

" The Iliad " [Bryant's translation], Book XXII, 375-378. Copied into his Diary, 1815.

307. Fate gave man the courage of endurance.

Diary, 1814.

308.
" *Portia*—How far that little candle throws his
        beams!
    So shines a good deed in a naughty
        world."

Marked in his copy of Shakespeare's " Merchant of Venice."

309. " And on the day that one becomes a
        slave
    The Thunderer, Jove, takes half his
        worth away."—Homer.

" The Odyssey " [Bryant's translation], Book XVII, 392-393. Marked by Beethoven.

310. " Short is the life of man, and whoso
bears
A cruel heart, devising cruel things,
On him men call down evil from the
gods
While living, and pursue him, when he
dies,
With scoffs. But whoso is of generous heart
And harbors generous aims, his guests
proclaim
His praises far and wide to all mankind,
And numberless are they who call him
good."—Homer.

"The Odyssey" [Bryant's translation], Book XIX,
408-415. Copied into his diary, 1818.

GOD

Beethoven was through and through a religious man though not in the confessional sense. Reared in the Catholic faith he early attained to an independent opinion on religious things. It must be borne in mind that his youth fell in the period of enlightenment and rationalism. When at a later date he composed the grand Mass in honor of his esteemed pupil Archduke Rudolph,—he hoped to obtain from him a chapelmastership when the Archduke became Archbishop of Olmütz, but in vain,—he gave it forms and dimensions which deviated from the ritual.

In all things liberty was the fundamental principle of Beethoven's life. His favorite book was Sturm's "Observations Concerning God's Works in Nature" (Betrachtungen über die Werke Gottes in der Natur), which he recommended to the priests for wide distribution among the people. He saw the hand of God in even the most insignificant natural phenomenon. God was to him the Supreme Being whom he had jubilantly hymned in the choral portion of the Ninth Symphony in the words of Schiller: "Brothers, beyond yon starry canopy there must dwell a loving Father!" Beethoven's relationship to God was that of a child

toward his loving father to whom he confides
all his joys as well as sorrows. It is said that
once he narrowly escaped excommunication for
having said that Jesus was only a poor human
being and a Jew. Haydn, ingenuously pious, is
reported to have called Beethoven an atheist.

He consented to the calling in of a priest on
his death-bed. Eye-witnesses testify that the
customary function was performed most impres-
sively and edifyingly and that Beethoven expressed his thanks to the officiating priest with
heartiness. After he had left the room Beethoven said to his friends: "*Plaudite, amici,
comoedia finita est*," the phrase with which antique dramas were concluded. From this fact
the statement has been made that Beethoven
wished to characterize the sacrament of extreme
unction as a comedy. This is contradicted,
however, by his conduct during its administra-
tion. It is more probable that he wished to
designate his life as a drama; in this sense, at
any rate, the words were accepted by his
friends. Schindler says emphatically: "The
last days were in all respects remarkable, and
he looked forward to death with truly Socratic
wisdom and peace of mind.

[I append a description of the death scene as I found
it in the note-books of A. W. Thayer which were placed
in my hands for examination after the death of Beethoven's greatest biographer in 1897. "June 5, 1860, I was
in Graz and saw Hüttenbrenner (Anselm) who gave me
the following particulars: .   .   .   In the winter of
1826-27 his friends wrote him from Vienna, that if he
wished to see Beethoven again alive he must hurry thither

from Graz. He hastened to Vienna, arriving a few days before Beethoven's death. Early in the afternoon of March 26, Hüttenbrenner went into the dying man's room. He mentioned as persons whom he saw there Stephen v. Breuning and Gerhard, Schindler, Telscher and Carl's mother (this seems to be a mistake, *i.e.* if Mrs. v. Beethoven is right). Beethoven had then long been senseless. Telscher began drawing the dying face of Beethoven. This grated on Breuning's feelings, and he remonstrated with him, and he put up his papers and left (?). Then Breuning and Schindler left to go out to Währing to select a grave. (Just after five—I got this from Breuning himself—when it grew dark with the sudden storm, Gerhard, who had been standing at the window, ran home to his teacher.) Afterward Gerhard v. B. went home, and there remained in the room only Hüttenbrenner and Mrs. van Beethoven. The storm passed over, covering the Glacis with snow and sleet. As it passed away a flash of lightning lighted up everything. This was followed by an awful clap of thunder. Hüttenbrenner had been sitting on the side of the bed sustaining Beethoven's head—holding it up with his right arm. His breathing was already very much impeded, and he had been for hours dying. At this startling, awful peal of thunder, the dying man suddenly raised his head from Hüttenbrenner's arm, stretched out his own right arm majestically—'like a general giving orders to an army.' This was but for an instant; the arm sunk back; he fell back. Beethoven was dead.

" Another talk with Hüttenbrenner. It seems that Beethoven was at his last gasp, one eye already closed. At the stroke of lightning and the thunder peal he raised his arm with a doubled-up fist; the expression of his eyes and face was that of one ' defying death,'—a look of defiance and power of resistance.

" He must have had his arm under the pillow. I must ask him.

" I did ask him; he had his arm around B.'s neck."
H. E. K.]

311. I am that which is. I am all that was, that is, and that shall be. No mortal man has ever lifted the veil of me. He is solely of him-

self, and to this Only One all things owe their
existence.

Beethoven's creed. He had found it in Champollion's
"The Paintings of Egypt," where it is set down as an
inscription on a temple to the goddess Neith. Beethoven
had his copy framed and kept it constantly before him on
his writing desk. "The relic was a great treasure in his
eyes." (Schindler.)

312. Wrapped in the shadows of eternal solitude, in the impenetrable darkness of the thicket,
impenetrable, immeasurable, unapproachable,
formlessly extended. Before spirit was breathed
(into things) his spirit was, and his only. As
mortal eyes (to compare finite and infinite
things) look into a shining mirror.

Copied, evidently, from an unidentified work, by Beethoven; though possibly original with him.

313. It was not the fortuitous meeting of the
chordal atoms that made the world; if order
and beauty are reflected in the constitution of
the universe, then there is a God.

Diary, 1816.

314. He who is above,—O, He is, and without Him there is nothing.

Diary.

315. Go to the devil with your "gracious
Sir!" There is only one who can be called
gracious, and that is God.

About 1824 or 1825, to Rampel, a copyist, who, ap-
parently, had been a little too obsequious in his address
to Beethoven. [As is customary among the Viennese to
this day. H. E. K.]

316. What is all this compared with the

great Tonemaster above! above! above! and
righteously the Most High, whereas here below
all is mockery,—dwarfs,—and yet Most High!!

To Schott, publisher in Mayence, in 1824—the same
year in which Beethoven copied the Egyptian inscription.

317. There is no loftier mission than to approach the Divinity nearer than other men, and
to disseminate the divine rays among mankind.

August, 1823, to Archduke Rudolph.

318. Heaven rules over the destiny of men
and monsters (literally, human and inhuman be-
ings), and so it will guide me, too, to the better
things of life.

September 11, 1811, to the poet Elsie von der Recke.

319. It's the same with humanity; here, too
(in suffering), he must show his strength, *i.e.*
endure without knowing or feeling his nullity,
and reach his perfection again for which the
Most High wishes to make us worthy.

May 13, 1816, to Countess Erdödy, who was suffering
from incurable lameness.

320. Religion and thorough-bass are settled
things concerning which there should be no dis-
puting.

Reported by Schindler.

321. All things flowed clear and pure out of
God. Though often darkly led to evil by pas-
sion, I returned, through penance and purifica-
tion to the pure fountain,—to God,—and to
your art. In this I was never impelled by self-
ishness; may it always be so. The trees bend

low under the weight of fruit, the clouds descend when they are filled with salutary rains, and the benefactors of humanity are not puffed up by their wealth.

Diary, 1815. The first portion seems to be a quotation, but Beethoven continues after the dash most characteristically in his own words and a change of person.

322. God is immaterial, and for this reason transcends every conception. Since He is invisible He can have no form. But from what we observe in His work we may conclude that He is eternal, omnipotent, omniscient and omnipresent.

Copied, with the remark: "From Indian literature" from an unidentified work, into the Diary of 1816.

323. In praise of Thy goodness I must confess that Thou didst try with all Thy means to draw me to Thee. Sometimes it pleased Thee to let me feel the heavy hand of Thy displeasure and to humiliate my proud heart by manifold castigations. Sickness and misfortune didst Thou send upon me to turn my thoughts to my errantries.—One thing, only, O Father, do I ask: cease not to labor for my betterment. In whatsoever manner it be, let me turn to Thee and become fruitful in good works.

Copied into the Diary from Sturm's book, "Observations Concerning the Works of God in Nature."

APPENDIX

Some observations may finally be acceptable touching Beethoven's general culture to which the thoughts of the reader must naturally have been directed by the excerpts from his writings set forth in the preceding pages. His own words betray the fact that he was not privileged to enjoy a thorough school-training and was thus compelled to the end of his days to make good the deficiencies in his learning. As a lad at Bonn he had attended the so-called Tirocinium, a sort of preparatory school for the Gymnasium, and acquired a small knowledge of Latin. Later he made great efforts to acquire French, a language essential to intercourse in the upper circles of society. He never established intimate relations with the rules of German. He used small initials for substantives, or capitalized verbs and adjectives according as they appeared important to him. His punctuation was arbitrary; generally he drew a perpendicular line between his words, letting it suffice for a comma or period as the case might be (a proceeding which adds not a little to the embarrassments of him who seeks to translate his sometimes mystical utterances).

It is said that a man's bookcase bears evidence of his education and intellectual interests.

Beethoven also had books,—not many, but a
characteristic collection. From his faithful
friend and voluntary servant Schindler we have
a report on this subject. Of the books of which
he was possessed at the time of his death there
have been preserved four volumes of translations of Shakespeare's works, Homer's " Odyssey " in the translation of J. H. Voss, Sturm's
" Observations " (several times referred to in
the preceding pages), and Goethe's " Westöstlichen Divan." These books are frequently
marked and annotated in lead pencil, thus bear-
ing witness to the subjects which interested Beethoven. From them, and volumes which he had
borrowed, many passages were copied by him
into his daily journal. Besides these books
Schindler mentions Homer's " Iliad," Goethe's
poems, "Wilhelm Meister " and " Faust," Schiller's dramas and poems, Tiedge's " Urania,"
volumes of poems by Matthisson and Seume,
and Nina d'Aubigny's " Letters to Natalia on
Singing,"—a book to which Beethoven attached
great value. These books have disappeared, as
well as others which Beethoven valued. We do
not know what became of the volumes of Plato,
Aristotle, Plutarch and Xenophon, or the writings of Pliny, Euripides, Quintilian, Ovid, Hor-
ace, Ossian, Milton and Thomson, traces of
which are found in Beethoven's utterances.
The catalogue made for the auction sale of his
posthumous effects on September 7, 1827, included forty-four works of which the censorship

seized five as prohibited writings, namely, Seume's " Foot Journey to Syracuse," the Apocrypha, Kotzebue's " On the Nobility," W. E. Müller's " Paris in its Zenith " (1816), and Fessler's " Views on Religion and Ecclesiasticism." Burney's " General History of Music " was also in his library, the gift, probably of an English admirer.

In his later years Beethoven was obliged to use the oft-quoted " Conversation-books " in his intercourse with friends and strangers alike who wrote down their questions. Of these little books Schindler preserved no less than 134, which are now in the Royal Library in Berlin. Naturally Beethoven answered the written questions orally as a rule. An idea of Beethoven's opinions can occasionally be gathered from the context of the questions, but frequently we are left in the dark.

Beethoven's own characterization of his deafness as " singular " is significant. Often, even in his later years, he was able to hear a little and for a time. One might almost speak of a periodical visitation of the " demon." In his biography Marx gives the following description of the malady: " As early as 1816 it is found that he is incapable of conducting his own works; in 1824 he could not hear the storm of applause from a great audience; but in 1822 he still improvises marvellously in social circles; in 1824 he studies their parts in the Ninth Symphony and Solemn Mass with Sontag and Un-

gher, and in 1825 he listens critically to a performance of the quartet in A-minor op. 132."
It is to be assumed that in such urgent cases his
will-power temporarily gave new tension to the
gradually atrophying aural nerves (it is said
that he was still able to hear single or a few
voices with his left ear but could not apprehend
masses), but this was not the case in less important moments, as the Conversation-books
prove. In these books a few answers are also
written down, naturally enough in cases not intended for the ears of strangers. At various
times Beethoven kept a diary in which he en-
tered his most intimate thoughts, especially
those designed for his own encouragement.
Many of these appear in the preceding pages.
In these instances more than in any others his
expressions are obscure, detached and, through
indifference, faulty in construction. For the
greater part they are remarks thrown upon the
paper in great haste.

A CATALOG OF SELECTED
DOVER BOOKS
IN ALL FIELDS OF INTEREST

A CATALOG OF SELECTED DOVER
BOOKS IN ALL FIELDS OF INTEREST

DRAWINGS OF REMBRANDT, edited by Seymour Slive. Updated Lippmann, Hofstede de Groot edition, with definitive scholarly apparatus. All portraits, biblical sketches, landscapes, nudes. Oriental figures, classical studies, together with selection of work by followers. 550 illustrations. Total of 630pp. 9⅛ × 12¼.
21485-0, 21486-9 Pa., Two-vol. set $25.00

GHOST AND HORROR STORIES OF AMBROSE BIERCE, Ambrose Bierce. 24 tales vividly imagined, strangely prophetic, and decades ahead of their time in technical skill: "The Damned Thing," "An Inhabitant of Carcosa," "The Eyes of the Panther," "Moxon's Master," and 20 more. 199pp. 5⅜ × 8½. 20767-6 Pa. $3.95

ETHICAL WRITINGS OF MAIMONIDES, Maimonides. Most significant ethical works of great medieval sage, newly translated for utmost precision, readability. Laws Concerning Character Traits, Eight Chapters, more. 192pp. 5⅜ × 8½.
24522-5 Pa. $4.50

THE EXPLORATION OF THE COLORADO RIVER AND ITS CANYONS, J. W. Powell. Full text of Powell's 1,000-mile expedition down the fabled Colorado in 1869. Superb account of terrain, geology, vegetation, Indians, famine, mutiny, treacherous rapids, mighty canyons, during exploration of last unknown part of continental U.S. 400pp. 5⅜ × 8½. 20094-9 Pa. $6.95

HISTORY OF PHILOSOPHY, Julián Marías. Clearest one-volume history on the market. Every major philosopher and dozens of others, to Existentialism and later. 505pp. 5⅜ × 8½. 21739-6 Pa. $8.50

ALL ABOUT LIGHTNING, Martin A. Uman. Highly readable non-technical survey of nature and causes of lightning, thunderstorms, ball lightning, St. Elmo's Fire, much more. Illustrated. 192pp. 5⅜ × 8½. 25237-X Pa. $5.95

SAILING ALONE AROUND THE WORLD, Captain Joshua Slocum. First man to sail around the world, alone, in small boat. One of great feats of seamanship told in delightful manner. 67 illustrations. 294pp. 5⅜ × 8½. 20326-3 Pa. $4.95

LETTERS AND NOTES ON THE MANNERS, CUSTOMS AND CONDITIONS OF THE NORTH AMERICAN INDIANS, George Catlin. Classic account of life among Plains Indians: ceremonies, hunt, warfare, etc. 312 plates. 572pp. of text. 6⅛ × 9¼. 22118-0, 22119-9 Pa. Two-vol. set $15.90

ALASKA: The Harriman Expedition, 1899, John Burroughs, John Muir, et al. Informative, engrossing accounts of two-month, 9,000-mile expedition. Native peoples, wildlife, forests, geography, salmon industry, glaciers, more. Profusely illustrated. 240 black-and-white line drawings. 124 black-and-white photographs. 3 maps. Index. 576pp. 5⅜ × 8½. 25109-8 Pa. $11.95

HOW TO WRITE, Gertrude Stein. Gertrude Stein claimed anyone could understand her unconventional writing—here are clues to help. Fascinating improvisations, language experiments, explanations illuminate Stein's craft and the art of writing. Total of 414pp. 4⅜ × 6⅜. 23144-5 Pa. $5.95

ADVENTURES AT SEA IN THE GREAT AGE OF SAIL: Five Firsthand Narratives, edited by Elliot Snow. Rare true accounts of exploration, whaling, shipwreck, fierce natives, trade, shipboard life, more. 33 illustrations. Introduction. 353pp. 5⅜ × 8½. 25177-2 Pa. $7.95

THE HERBAL OR GENERAL HISTORY OF PLANTS, John Gerard. Classic descriptions of about 2,850 plants—with over 2,700 illustrations—includes Latin and English names, physical descriptions, varieties, time and place of growth, more. 2,706 illustrations. xlv + 1,678pp. 8½ × 12¼. 23147-X Cloth. $75.00

DOROTHY AND THE WIZARD IN OZ, L. Frank Baum. Dorothy and the Wizard visit the center of the Earth, where people are vegetables, glass houses grow and Oz characters reappear. Classic sequel to *Wizard of Oz*. 256pp. 5⅜ × 8. 24714-7 Pa. $4.95

SONGS OF EXPERIENCE: Facsimile Reproduction with 26 Plates in Full Color, William Blake. This facsimile of Blake's original "Illuminated Book" reproduces 26 full-color plates from a rare 1826 edition. Includes "The Tyger," "London," "Holy Thursday," and other immortal poems. 26 color plates. Printed text of poems. 48pp. 5¼ × 7. 24636-1 Pa. $3.50

SONGS OF INNOCENCE, William Blake. The first and most popular of Blake's famous "Illuminated Books," in a facsimile edition reproducing all 31 brightly colored plates. Additional printed text of each poem. 64pp. 5¼ × 7. 22764-2 Pa. $3.50

PRECIOUS STONES, Max Bauer. Classic, thorough study of diamonds, rubies, emeralds, garnets, etc.: physical character, occurrence, properties, use, similar topics. 20 plates, 8 in color. 94 figures. 659pp. 6⅛ × 9¼. 21910-0, 21911-9 Pa., Two-vol. set $15.90

ENCYCLOPEDIA OF VICTORIAN NEEDLEWORK, S. F. A. Caulfeild and Blanche Saward. Full, precise descriptions of stitches, techniques for dozens of needlecrafts—most exhaustive reference of its kind. Over 800 figures. Total of 679pp. 8⅛ × 11. Two volumes. Vol. 1 22800-2 Pa. $11.95
Vol. 2 22801-0 Pa. $11.95

THE MARVELOUS LAND OF OZ, L. Frank Baum. Second Oz book, the Scarecrow and Tin Woodman are back with hero named Tip, Oz magic. 136 illustrations. 287pp. 5⅜ × 8½. 20692-0 Pa. $5.95

WILD FOWL DECOYS, Joel Barber. Basic book on the subject, by foremost authority and collector. Reveals history of decoy making and rigging, place in American culture, different kinds of decoys, how to make them, and how to use them. 140 plates. 156pp. 7⅞ × 10¾. 20011-6 Pa. $8.95

HISTORY OF LACE, Mrs. Bury Palliser. Definitive, profusely illustrated chronicle of lace from earliest times to late 19th century. Laces of Italy, Greece, England, France, Belgium, etc. Landmark of needlework scholarship. 266 illustrations. 672pp. 6⅛ × 9¼. 24742-2 Pa. $14.95

ILLUSTRATED GUIDE TO SHAKER FURNITURE, Robert Meader. All furniture and appurtenances, with much on unknown local styles. 235 photos. 146pp. 9 × 12. 22819-3 Pa. $7.95

WHALE SHIPS AND WHALING: A Pictorial Survey, George Francis Dow. Over 200 vintage engravings, drawings, photographs of barks, brigs, cutters, other vessels. Also harpoons, lances, whaling guns, many other artifacts. Comprehensive text by foremost authority. 207 black-and-white illustrations. 288pp. 6 × 9. 24808-9 Pa. $8.95

THE BERTRAMS, Anthony Trollope. Powerful portrayal of blind self-will and thwarted ambition includes one of Trollope's most heartrending love stories. 497pp. 5⅜ × 8½. 25119-5 Pa. $8.95

ADVENTURES WITH A HAND LENS, Richard Headstrom. Clearly written guide to observing and studying flowers and grasses, fish scales, moth and insect wings, egg cases, buds, feathers, seeds, leaf scars, moss, molds, ferns, common crystals, etc.—all with an ordinary, inexpensive magnifying glass. 209 exact line drawings aid in your discoveries. 220pp. 5⅜ × 8½. 23330-8 Pa. $4.50

RODIN ON ART AND ARTISTS, Auguste Rodin. Great sculptor's candid, wide-ranging comments on meaning of art; great artists; relation of sculpture to poetry, painting, music; philosophy of life, more. 76 superb black-and-white illustrations of Rodin's sculpture, drawings and prints. 119pp. 8⅜ × 11¼. 24487-3 Pa. $6.95

FIFTY CLASSIC FRENCH FILMS, 1912–1982: A Pictorial Record, Anthony Slide. Memorable stills from Grand Illusion, Beauty and the Beast, Hiroshima, Mon Amour, many more. Credits, plot synopses, reviews, etc. 160pp. 8¼ × 11. 25256-6 Pa. $11.95

THE PRINCIPLES OF PSYCHOLOGY, William James. Famous long course complete, unabridged. Stream of thought, time perception, memory, experimental methods; great work decades ahead of its time. 94 figures. 1,391pp. 5⅜ × 8½. 20381-6, 20382-4 Pa., Two-vol. set $19.90

BODIES IN A BOOKSHOP, R. T. Campbell. Challenging mystery of blackmail and murder with ingenious plot and superbly drawn characters. In the best tradition of British suspense fiction. 192pp. 5⅜ × 8½. 24720-1 Pa. $3.95

CALLAS: PORTRAIT OF A PRIMA DONNA, George Jellinek. Renowned commentator on the musical scene chronicles incredible career and life of the most controversial, fascinating, influential operatic personality of our time. 64 black-and-white photographs. 416pp. 5⅜ × 8¼. 25047-4 Pa. $7.95

GEOMETRY, RELATIVITY AND THE FOURTH DIMENSION, Rudolph Rucker. Exposition of fourth dimension, concepts of relativity as Flatland characters continue adventures. Popular, easily followed yet accurate, profound. 141 illustrations. 133pp. 5⅜ × 8½. 23400-2 Pa. $3.50

HOUSEHOLD STORIES BY THE BROTHERS GRIMM, with pictures by Walter Crane. 53 classic stories—Rumpelstiltskin, Rapunzel, Hansel and Gretel, the Fisherman and his Wife, Snow White, Tom Thumb, Sleeping Beauty, Cinderella, and so much more—lavishly illustrated with original 19th century drawings. 114 illustrations. x + 269pp. 5⅜ × 8½. 21080-4 Pa. $4.50

SUNDIALS, Albert Waugh. Far and away the best, most thorough coverage of ideas, mathematics concerned, types, construction, adjusting anywhere. Over 100 illustrations. 230pp. 5⅜ × 8½. 22947-5 Pa. $4.50

PICTURE HISTORY OF THE NORMANDIE: With 190 Illustrations, Frank O. Braynard. Full story of legendary French ocean liner: Art Deco interiors, design innovations, furnishings, celebrities, maiden voyage, tragic fire, much more. Extensive text. 144pp. 8⅜ × 11¾. 25257-4 Pa. $9.95

THE FIRST AMERICAN COOKBOOK: A Facsimile of "American Cookery," 1796, Amelia Simmons. Facsimile of the first American-written cookbook published in the United States contains authentic recipes for colonial favorites— pumpkin pudding, winter squash pudding, spruce beer, Indian slapjacks, and more. Introductory Essay and Glossary of colonial cooking terms. 80pp. 5⅜ × 8½. 24710-4 Pa. $3.50

101 PUZZLES IN THOUGHT AND LOGIC, C. R. Wylie, Jr. Solve murders and robberies, find out which fishermen are liars, how a blind man could possibly identify a color—purely by your own reasoning! 107pp. 5⅜ × 8½. 20367-0 Pa. $2.50

THE BOOK OF WORLD-FAMOUS MUSIC—CLASSICAL, POPULAR AND FOLK, James J. Fuld. Revised and enlarged republication of landmark work in musico-bibliography. Full information about nearly 1,000 songs and compositions including first lines of music and lyrics. New supplement. Index. 800pp. 5⅜ × 8¼. 24857-7 Pa. $14.95

ANTHROPOLOGY AND MODERN LIFE, Franz Boas. Great anthropologist's classic treatise on race and culture. Introduction by Ruth Bunzel. Only inexpensive paperback edition. 255pp. 5⅜ × 8½. 25245-0 Pa. $5.95

THE TALE OF PETER RABBIT, Beatrix Potter. The inimitable Peter's terrifying adventure in Mr. McGregor's garden, with all 27 wonderful, full-color Potter illustrations. 55pp. 4¼ × 5½. (Available in U.S. only) 22827-4 Pa. $1.75

THREE PROPHETIC SCIENCE FICTION NOVELS, H. G. Wells. *When the Sleeper Wakes, A Story of the Days to Come* and *The Time Machine* (full version). 335pp. 5⅜ × 8½. (Available in U.S. only) 20605-X Pa. $5.95

APICIUS COOKERY AND DINING IN IMPERIAL ROME, edited and translated by Joseph Dommers Vehling. Oldest known cookbook in existence offers readers a clear picture of what foods Romans ate, how they prepared them, etc. 49 illustrations. 301pp. 6⅛ × 9¼. 23563-7 Pa. $6.50

SHAKESPEARE LEXICON AND QUOTATION DICTIONARY, Alexander Schmidt. Full definitions, locations, shades of meaning of every word in plays and poems. More than 50,000 exact quotations. 1,485pp. 6½ × 9¼. 22726-X, 22727-8 Pa., Two-vol. set $27.90

THE WORLD'S GREAT SPEECHES, edited by Lewis Copeland and Lawrence W. Lamm. Vast collection of 278 speeches from Greeks to 1970. Powerful and effective models; unique look at history. 842pp. 5⅜ × 8½. 20468-5 Pa. $11.95

CATALOG OF DOVER BOOKS

THE BLUE FAIRY BOOK, Andrew Lang. The first, most famous collection, with many familiar tales: Little Red Riding Hood, Aladdin and the Wonderful Lamp, Puss in Boots, Sleeping Beauty, Hansel and Gretel, Rumpelstiltskin; 37 in all. 138 illustrations. 390pp. 5⅜ × 8½. 21437-0 Pa. $5.95

THE STORY OF THE CHAMPIONS OF THE ROUND TABLE, Howard Pyle. Sir Launcelot, Sir Tristram and Sir Percival in spirited adventures of love and triumph retold in Pyle's inimitable style. 50 drawings, 31 full-page. xviii + 329pp. 6½ × 9¼. 21883-X Pa. $6.95

AUDUBON AND HIS JOURNALS, Maria Audubon. Unmatched two-volume portrait of the great artist, naturalist and author contains his journals, an excellent biography by his granddaughter, expert annotations by the noted ornithologist, Dr. Elliott Coues, and 37 superb illustrations. Total of 1,200pp. 5⅜ × 8.
Vol. I 25143-8 Pa. $8.95
Vol. II 25144-6 Pa. $8.95

GREAT DINOSAUR HUNTERS AND THEIR DISCOVERIES, Edwin H. Colbert. Fascinating, lavishly illustrated chronicle of dinosaur research, 1820's to 1960. Achievements of Cope, Marsh, Brown, Buckland, Mantell, Huxley, many others. 384pp. 5¼ × 8¼. 24701-5 Pa. $6.95

THE TASTEMAKERS, Russell Lynes. Informal, illustrated social history of American taste 1850's–1950's. First popularized categories Highbrow, Lowbrow, Middlebrow. 129 illustrations. New (1979) afterword. 384pp. 6 × 9.
23993-4 Pa. $6.95

DOUBLE CROSS PURPOSES, Ronald A. Knox. A treasure hunt in the Scottish Highlands, an old map, unidentified corpse, surprise discoveries keep reader guessing in this cleverly intricate tale of financial skullduggery. 2 black-and-white maps. 320pp. 5⅜ × 8½. (Available in U.S. only) 25032-6 Pa. $5.95

AUTHENTIC VICTORIAN DECORATION AND ORNAMENTATION IN FULL COLOR: 46 Plates from "Studies in Design," Christopher Dresser. Superb full-color lithographs reproduced from rare original portfolio of a major Victorian designer. 48pp. 9¼ × 12¼. 25083-0 Pa. $7.95

PRIMITIVE ART, Franz Boas. Remains the best text ever prepared on subject, thoroughly discussing Indian, African, Asian, Australian, and, especially, Northern American primitive art. Over 950 illustrations show ceramics, masks, totem poles, weapons, textiles, paintings, much more. 376pp. 5⅜ × 8. 20025-6 Pa. $6.95

SIDELIGHTS ON RELATIVITY, Albert Einstein. Unabridged republication of two lectures delivered by the great physicist in 1920–21. *Ether and Relativity* and *Geometry and Experience*. Elegant ideas in non-mathematical form, accessible to intelligent layman. vi + 56pp. 5⅜ × 8½. 24511-X Pa. $2.95

THE WIT AND HUMOR OF OSCAR WILDE, edited by Alvin Redman. More than 1,000 ripostes, paradoxes, wisecracks: Work is the curse of the drinking classes, I can resist everything except temptation, etc. 258pp. 5⅜ × 8½. 20602-5 Pa. $4.50

ADVENTURES WITH A MICROSCOPE, Richard Headstrom. 59 adventures with clothing fibers, protozoa, ferns and lichens, roots and leaves, much more. 142 illustrations. 232pp. 5⅜ × 8½. 23471-1 Pa. $3.95

CATALOG OF DOVER BOOKS

PLANTS OF THE BIBLE, Harold N. Moldenke and Alma L. Moldenke. Standard reference to all 230 plants mentioned in Scriptures. Latin name, biblical reference, uses, modern identity, much more. Unsurpassed encyclopedic resource for scholars, botanists, nature lovers, students of Bible. Bibliography. Indexes. 123 black-and-white illustrations. 384pp. 6 × 9. 25069-5 Pa. $8.95

FAMOUS AMERICAN WOMEN: A Biographical Dictionary from Colonial Times to the Present, Robert McHenry, ed. From Pocahontas to Rosa Parks, 1,035 distinguished American women documented in separate biographical entries. Accurate, up-to-date data, numerous categories, spans 400 years. Indices. 493pp. 6½ × 9¼. 24523-3 Pa. $9.95

THE FABULOUS INTERIORS OF THE GREAT OCEAN LINERS IN HISTORIC PHOTOGRAPHS, William H. Miller, Jr. Some 200 superb photographs capture exquisite interiors of world's great "floating palaces"—1890's to 1980's: *Titanic, Ile de France, Queen Elizabeth, United States, Europa,* more. Approx. 200 black-and-white photographs. Captions. Text. Introduction. 160pp. 8⅜ × 11¼. 24756-2 Pa. $9.95

THE GREAT LUXURY LINERS, 1927-1954: A Photographic Record, William H. Miller, Jr. Nostalgic tribute to heyday of ocean liners. 186 photos of Ile de France, Normandie, Leviathan, Queen Elizabeth, United States, many others. Interior and exterior views. Introduction. Captions. 160pp. 9 × 12. 24056-8 Pa. $9.95

A NATURAL HISTORY OF THE DUCKS, John Charles Phillips. Great landmark of ornithology offers complete detailed coverage of nearly 200 species and subspecies of ducks: gadwall, sheldrake, merganser, pintail, many more. 74 full-color plates, 102 black-and-white. Bibliography. Total of 1,920pp. 8⅜ × 11¼. 25141-1, 25142-X Cloth. Two-vol. set $100.00

THE SEAWEED HANDBOOK: An Illustrated Guide to Seaweeds from North Carolina to Canada, Thomas F. Lee. Concise reference covers 78 species. Scientific and common names, habitat, distribution, more. Finding keys for easy identification. 224pp. 5⅜ × 8½. 25215-9 Pa. $5.95

THE TEN BOOKS OF ARCHITECTURE: The 1755 Leoni Edition, Leon Battista Alberti. Rare classic helped introduce the glories of ancient architecture to the Renaissance. 68 black-and-white plates. 336pp. 8⅜ × 11¼. 25239-6 Pa. $14.95

MISS MACKENZIE, Anthony Trollope. Minor masterpieces by Victorian master unmasks many truths about life in 19th-century England. First inexpensive edition in years. 392pp. 5⅜ × 8½. 25201-9 Pa. $7.95

THE RIME OF THE ANCIENT MARINER, Gustave Doré, Samuel Taylor Coleridge. Dramatic engravings considered by many to be his greatest work. The terrifying space of the open sea, the storms and whirlpools of an unknown ocean, the ice of Antarctica, more—all rendered in a powerful, chilling manner. Full text. 38 plates. 77pp. 9¼ × 12. 22305-1 Pa. $4.95

THE EXPEDITIONS OF ZEBULON MONTGOMERY PIKE, Zebulon Montgomery Pike. Fascinating first-hand accounts (1805-6) of exploration of Mississippi River, Indian wars, capture by Spanish dragoons, much more. 1,088pp. 5⅜ × 8½. 25254-X, 25255-8 Pa. Two-vol. set $23.90

CATALOG OF DOVER BOOKS

A CONCISE HISTORY OF PHOTOGRAPHY: Third Revised Edition, Helmut Gernsheim. Best one-volume history—camera obscura, photochemistry, daguerreotypes, evolution of cameras, film, more. Also artistic aspects—landscape, portraits, fine art, etc. 281 black-and-white photographs. 26 in color. 176pp. 8⅜ × 11¼. 25128-4 Pa. $12.95

THE DORÉ BIBLE ILLUSTRATIONS, Gustave Doré. 241 detailed plates from the Bible: the Creation scenes, Adam and Eve, Flood, Babylon, battle sequences, life of Jesus, etc. Each plate is accompanied by the verses from the King James version of the Bible. 241pp. 9 × 12. 23004-X Pa. $8.95

HUGGER-MUGGER IN THE LOUVRE, Elliot Paul. Second Homer Evans mystery-comedy. Theft at the Louvre involves sleuth in hilarious, madcap caper. "A knockout."—Books. 336pp. 5⅜ × 8½. 25185-3 Pa. $5.95

FLATLAND, E. A. Abbott. Intriguing and enormously popular science-fiction classic explores the complexities of trying to survive as a two-dimensional being in a three-dimensional world. Amusingly illustrated by the author. 16 illustrations. 103pp. 5⅜ × 8½. 20001-9 Pa. $2.25

THE HISTORY OF THE LEWIS AND CLARK EXPEDITION, Meriwether Lewis and William Clark, edited by Elliott Coues. Classic edition of Lewis and Clark's day-by-day journals that later became the basis for U.S. claims to Oregon and the West. Accurate and invaluable geographical, botanical, biological, meteorological and anthropological material. Total of 1,508pp. 5⅜ × 8½.
21268-8, 21269-6, 21270-X Pa. Three-vol. set $25.50

LANGUAGE, TRUTH AND LOGIC, Alfred J. Ayer. Famous, clear introduction to Vienna, Cambridge schools of Logical Positivism. Role of philosophy, elimination of metaphysics, nature of analysis, etc. 160pp. 5⅜ × 8½. (Available in U.S. and Canada only) 20010-8 Pa. $2.95

MATHEMATICS FOR THE NONMATHEMATICIAN, Morris Kline. Detailed, college-level treatment of mathematics in cultural and historical context, with numerous exercises. For liberal arts students. Preface. Recommended Reading Lists. Tables. Index. Numerous black-and-white figures. xvi + 641pp. 5⅜ × 8½. 24823-2 Pa. $11.95

28 SCIENCE FICTION STORIES, H. G. Wells. Novels, *Star Begotten* and *Men Like Gods*, plus 26 short stories: "Empire of the Ants," "A Story of the Stone Age," "The Stolen Bacillus," "In the Abyss," etc. 915pp. 5⅜ × 8½. (Available in U.S. only) 20265-8 Cloth. $10.95

HANDBOOK OF PICTORIAL SYMBOLS, Rudolph Modley. 3,250 signs and symbols, many systems in full; official or heavy commercial use. Arranged by subject. Most in Pictorial Archive series. 143pp. 8⅜ × 11. 23357-X Pa. $5.95

INCIDENTS OF TRAVEL IN YUCATAN, John L. Stephens. Classic (1843) exploration of jungles of Yucatan, looking for evidences of Maya civilization. Travel adventures, Mexican and Indian culture, etc. Total of 669pp. 5⅜ × 8½.
20926-1, 20927-X Pa., Two-vol. set $9.90

CATALOG OF DOVER BOOKS

DEGAS: An Intimate Portrait, Ambroise Vollard. Charming, anecdotal memoir by famous art dealer of one of the greatest 19th-century French painters. 14 black-and-white illustrations. Introduction by Harold L. Van Doren. 96pp. 5⅜ × 8½.
25131-4 Pa. $3.95

PERSONAL NARRATIVE OF A PILGRIMAGE TO ALMANDINAH AND MECCAH, Richard Burton. Great travel classic by remarkably colorful personality. Burton, disguised as a Moroccan, visited sacred shrines of Islam, narrowly escaping death. 47 illustrations. 959pp. 5⅜ × 8½. 21217-3, 21218-1 Pa., Two-vol. set $17.90

PHRASE AND WORD ORIGINS, A. H. Holt. Entertaining, reliable, modern study of more than 1,200 colorful words, phrases, origins and histories. Much unexpected information. 254pp. 5⅜ × 8½. 20758-7 Pa. $5.95

THE RED THUMB MARK, R. Austin Freeman. In this first Dr. Thorndyke case, the great scientific detective draws fascinating conclusions from the nature of a single fingerprint. Exciting story, authentic science. 320pp. 5⅜ × 8½. (Available in U.S. only) 25210-8 Pa. $5.95

AN EGYPTIAN HIEROGLYPHIC DICTIONARY, E. A. Wallis Budge. Monumental work containing about 25,000 words or terms that occur in texts ranging from 3000 B.C. to 600 A.D. Each entry consists of a transliteration of the word, the word in hieroglyphs, and the meaning in English. 1,314pp. 6⅜ × 10.
23615-3, 23616-1 Pa., Two-vol. set $27.90

THE COMPLEAT STRATEGYST: Being a Primer on the Theory of Games of Strategy, J. D. Williams. Highly entertaining classic describes, with many illustrated examples, how to select best strategies in conflict situations. Prefaces. Appendices. xvi + 268pp. 5⅜ × 8½. 25101-2 Pa. $5.95

THE ROAD TO OZ, L. Frank Baum. Dorothy meets the Shaggy Man, little Button-Bright and the Rainbow's beautiful daughter in this delightful trip to the magical Land of Oz. 272pp. 5⅜ × 8. 25208-6 Pa. $4.95

POINT AND LINE TO PLANE, Wassily Kandinsky. Seminal exposition of role of point, line, other elements in non-objective painting. Essential to understanding 20th-century art. 127 illustrations. 192pp. 6½ × 9¼. 23808-3 Pa. $4.50

LADY ANNA, Anthony Trollope. Moving chronicle of Countess Lovel's bitter struggle to win for herself and daughter Anna their rightful rank and fortune—perhaps at cost of sanity itself. 384pp. 5⅜ × 8½. 24669-8 Pa. $6.95

EGYPTIAN MAGIC, E. A. Wallis Budge. Sums up all that is known about magic in Ancient Egypt: the role of magic in controlling the gods, powerful amulets that warded off evil spirits, scarabs of immortality, use of wax images, formulas and spells, the secret name, much more. 253pp. 5⅜ × 8½. 22681-6 Pa. $4.50

THE DANCE OF SIVA, Ananda Coomaraswamy. Preeminent authority unfolds the vast metaphysic of India: the revelation of her art, conception of the universe, social organization, etc. 27 reproductions of art masterpieces. 192pp. 5⅜ × 8½.
24817-8 Pa. $5.95

CATALOG OF DOVER BOOKS

CHRISTMAS CUSTOMS AND TRADITIONS, Clement A. Miles. Origin, evolution, significance of religious, secular practices. Caroling, gifts, yule logs, much more. Full, scholarly yet fascinating; non-sectarian. 400pp. 5⅜ × 8½.
23354-5 Pa. $6.50

THE HUMAN FIGURE IN MOTION, Eadweard Muybridge. More than 4,500 stopped-action photos, in action series, showing undraped men, women, children jumping, lying down, throwing, sitting, wrestling, carrying, etc. 390pp. 7⅞ × 10⅝.
20204-6 Cloth. $19.95

THE MAN WHO WAS THURSDAY, Gilbert Keith Chesterton. Witty, fast-paced novel about a club of anarchists in turn-of-the-century London. Brilliant social, religious, philosophical speculations. 128pp. 5⅜ × 8½.
25121-7 Pa. $3.95

A CEZANNE SKETCHBOOK: Figures, Portraits, Landscapes and Still Lifes, Paul Cezanne. Great artist experiments with tonal effects, light, mass, other qualities in over 100 drawings. A revealing view of developing master painter, precursor of Cubism. 102 black-and-white illustrations. 144pp. 8¾ × 6⅝.
24790-2 Pa. $5.95

AN ENCYCLOPEDIA OF BATTLES: Accounts of Over 1,560 Battles from 1479 B.C. to the Present, David Eggenberger. Presents essential details of every major battle in recorded history, from the first battle of Megiddo in 1479 B.C. to Grenada in 1984. List of Battle Maps. New Appendix covering the years 1967–1984. Index. 99 illustrations. 544pp. 6½ × 9¼.
24913-1 Pa. $14.95

AN ETYMOLOGICAL DICTIONARY OF MODERN ENGLISH, Ernest Weekley. Richest, fullest work, by foremost British lexicographer. Detailed word histories. Inexhaustible. Total of 856pp. 6½ × 9¼.
21873-2, 21874-0 Pa., Two-vol. set $17.00

WEBSTER'S AMERICAN MILITARY BIOGRAPHIES, edited by Robert McHenry. Over 1,000 figures who shaped 3 centuries of American military history. Detailed biographies of Nathan Hale, Douglas MacArthur, Mary Hallaren, others. Chronologies of engagements, more. Introduction. Addenda. 1,033 entries in alphabetical order. xi + 548pp. 6½ × 9¼. (Available in U.S. only)
24758-9 Pa. $11.95

LIFE IN ANCIENT EGYPT, Adolf Erman. Detailed older account, with much not in more recent books: domestic life, religion, magic, medicine, commerce, and whatever else needed for complete picture. Many illustrations. 597pp. 5⅜ × 8½.
22632-8 Pa. $8.95

HISTORIC COSTUME IN PICTURES, Braun & Schneider. Over 1,450 costumed figures shown, covering a wide variety of peoples: kings, emperors, nobles, priests, servants, soldiers, scholars, townsfolk, peasants, merchants, courtiers, cavaliers, and more. 256pp. 8⅜ × 11¼.
23150-X Pa. $7.95

THE NOTEBOOKS OF LEONARDO DA VINCI, edited by J. P. Richter. Extracts from manuscripts reveal great genius; on painting, sculpture, anatomy, sciences, geography, etc. Both Italian and English. 186 ms. pages reproduced, plus 500 additional drawings, including studies for *Last Supper, Sforza* monument, etc. 860pp. 7⅞ × 10¾. (Available in U.S. only) 22572-0, 22573-9 Pa., Two-vol. set $25.90

THE ART NOUVEAU STYLE BOOK OF ALPHONSE MUCHA: All 72 Plates from "Documents Decoratifs" in Original Color, Alphonse Mucha. Rare copyright-free design portfolio by high priest of Art Nouveau. Jewelry, wallpaper, stained glass, furniture, figure studies, plant and animal motifs, etc. Only complete one-volume edition. 80pp. 9⅜ × 12¼. 24044-4 Pa. $8.95

ANIMALS: 1,419 COPYRIGHT-FREE ILLUSTRATIONS OF MAMMALS, BIRDS, FISH, INSECTS, ETC., edited by Jim Harter. Clear wood engravings present, in extremely lifelike poses, over 1,000 species of animals. One of the most extensive pictorial sourcebooks of its kind. Captions. Index. 284pp. 9 × 12.
23766-4 Pa. $9.95

OBELISTS FLY HIGH, C. Daly King. Masterpiece of American detective fiction, long out of print, involves murder on a 1935 transcontinental flight—"a very thrilling story"—NY Times. Unabridged and unaltered republication of the edition published by William Collins Sons & Co. Ltd., London, 1935. 288pp. 5⅜ × 8½. (Available in U.S. only) 25036-9 Pa. $4.95

VICTORIAN AND EDWARDIAN FASHION: A Photographic Survey, Alison Gernsheim. First fashion history completely illustrated by contemporary photographs. Full text plus 235 photos, 1840-1914, in which many celebrities appear. 240pp. 6½ × 9¼. 24205-6 Pa. $6.00

THE ART OF THE FRENCH ILLUSTRATED BOOK, 1700-1914, Gordon N. Ray. Over 630 superb book illustrations by Fragonard, Delacroix, Daumier, Doré, Grandville, Manet, Mucha, Steinlen, Toulouse-Lautrec and many others. Preface. Introduction. 633 halftones. Indices of artists, authors & titles, binders and provenances. Appendices. Bibliography. 608pp. 8⅜ × 11¼. 25086-5 Pa. $24.95

THE WONDERFUL WIZARD OF OZ, L. Frank Baum. Facsimile in full color of America's finest children's classic. 143 illustrations by W. W. Denslow. 267pp. 5⅜ × 8½. 20691-2 Pa. $5.95

FRONTIERS OF MODERN PHYSICS: New Perspectives on Cosmology, Relativity, Black Holes and Extraterrestrial Intelligence, Tony Rothman, et al. For the intelligent layman. Subjects include: cosmological models of the universe; black holes; the neutrino; the search for extraterrestrial intelligence. Introduction. 46 black-and-white illustrations. 192pp. 5⅜ × 8½. 24587-X Pa. $6.95

THE FRIENDLY STARS, Martha Evans Martin & Donald Howard Menzel. Classic text marshalls the stars together in an engaging, non-technical survey, presenting them as sources of beauty in night sky. 23 illustrations. Foreword. 2 star charts. Index. 147pp. 5⅜ × 8½. 21099-5 Pa. $3.50

FADS AND FALLACIES IN THE NAME OF SCIENCE, Martin Gardner. Fair, witty appraisal of cranks, quacks, and quackeries of science and pseudoscience: hollow earth, Velikovsky, orgone energy, Dianetics, flying saucers, Bridey Murphy, food and medical fads, etc. Revised, expanded In the Name of Science. "A very able and even-tempered presentation."—The New Yorker. 363pp. 5⅜ × 8. 20394-8 Pa. $6.50

ANCIENT EGYPT: ITS CULTURE AND HISTORY, J. E Manchip White. From pre-dynastics through Ptolemies: society, history, political structure, religion, daily life, literature, cultural heritage. 48 plates. 217pp. 5⅜ × 8½. 22548-8 Pa. $4.95

CATALOG OF DOVER BOOKS

SIR HARRY HOTSPUR OF HUMBLETHWAITE, Anthony Trollope. Incisive, unconventional psychological study of a conflict between a wealthy baronet, his idealistic daughter, and their scapegrace cousin. The 1870 novel in its first inexpensive edition in years. 250pp. 5⅜ × 8½. 24953-0 Pa. $5.95

LASERS AND HOLOGRAPHY, Winston E. Kock. Sound introduction to burgeoning field, expanded (1981) for second edition. Wave patterns, coherence, lasers, diffraction, zone plates, properties of holograms, recent advances. 84 illustrations. 160pp. 5⅜ × 8¼. (Except in United Kingdom) 24041-X Pa. $3.50

INTRODUCTION TO ARTIFICIAL INTELLIGENCE: SECOND, EN-LARGED EDITION, Philip C. Jackson, Jr. Comprehensive survey of artificial intelligence—the study of how machines (computers) can be made to act intelligently. Includes introductory and advanced material. Extensive notes updating the main text. 132 black-and-white illustrations. 512pp. 5⅜ × 8½. 24864-X Pa. $8.95

HISTORY OF INDIAN AND INDONESIAN ART, Ananda K. Coomaraswamy. Over 400 illustrations illuminate classic study of Indian art from earliest Harappa finds to early 20th century. Provides philosophical, religious and social insights. 304pp. 6⅜ × 9⅜. 25005-9 Pa. $8.95

THE GOLEM, Gustav Meyrink. Most famous supernatural novel in modern European literature, set in Ghetto of Old Prague around 1890. Compelling story of mystical experiences, strange transformations, profound terror. 13 black-and-white illustrations. 224pp. 5⅜ × 8½. (Available in U.S. only) 25025-3 Pa. $5.95

ARMADALE, Wilkie Collins. Third great mystery novel by the author of *The Woman in White* and *The Moonstone*. Original magazine version with 40 illustrations. 597pp. 5⅜ × 8½. 23429-0 Pa. $9.95

PICTORIAL ENCYCLOPEDIA OF HISTORIC ARCHITECTURAL PLANS, DETAILS AND ELEMENTS: With 1,880 Line Drawings of Arches, Domes, Doorways, Facades, Gables, Windows, etc., John Theodore Haneman. Sourcebook of inspiration for architects, designers, others. Bibliography. Captions. 141pp. 9 × 12. 24605-1 Pa. $6.95

BENCHLEY LOST AND FOUND, Robert Benchley. Finest humor from early 30's, about pet peeves, child psychologists, post office and others. Mostly unavailable elsewhere. 73 illustrations by Peter Arno and others. 183pp. 5⅜ × 8½. 22410-4 Pa. $3.95

ERTÉ GRAPHICS, Erté. Collection of striking color graphics: *Seasons, Alphabet, Numerals, Aces* and *Precious Stones*. 50 plates, including 4 on covers. 48pp. 9⅜ × 12¼. 23580-7 Pa. $6.95

THE JOURNAL OF HENRY D. THOREAU, edited by Bradford Torrey, F. H. Allen. Complete reprinting of 14 volumes, 1837–61, over two million words; the sourcebooks for *Walden*, etc. Definitive. All original sketches, plus 75 photographs. 1,804pp. 8½ × 12¼. 20312-3, 20313-1 Cloth., Two-vol. set $80.00

CASTLES: THEIR CONSTRUCTION AND HISTORY, Sidney Toy. Traces castle development from ancient roots. Nearly 200 photographs and drawings illustrate moats, keeps, baileys, many other features. Caernarvon, Dover Castles, Hadrian's Wall, Tower of London, dozens more. 256pp. 5⅜ × 8¼. 24898-4 Pa. $5.95

CATALOG OF DOVER BOOKS

AMERICAN CLIPPER SHIPS: 1833–1858, Octavius T. Howe & Frederick C. Matthews. Fully-illustrated, encyclopedic review of 352 clipper ships from the period of America's greatest maritime supremacy. Introduction. 109 halftones. 5 black-and-white line illustrations. Index. Total of 928pp. 5⅜ × 8½.
25115-2, 25116-0 Pa., Two-vol. set $17.90

TOWARDS A NEW ARCHITECTURE, Le Corbusier. Pioneering manifesto by great architect, near legendary founder of "International School." Technical and aesthetic theories, views on industry, economics, relation of form to function, "mass-production spirit," much more. Profusely illustrated. Unabridged translation of 13th French edition. Introduction by Frederick Etchells. 320pp. 6⅛ × 9¼.
(Available in U.S. only)   25023-7 Pa. $8.95

THE BOOK OF KELLS, edited by Blanche Cirker. Inexpensive collection of 32 full-color, full-page plates from the greatest illuminated manuscript of the Middle Ages, painstakingly reproduced from rare facsimile edition. Publisher's Note. Captions. 32pp. 9⅜ × 12¼.   24345-1 Pa. $4.95

BEST SCIENCE FICTION STORIES OF H. G. WELLS, H. G. Wells. Full novel *The Invisible Man*, plus 17 short stories: "The Crystal Egg," "Aepyornis Island," "The Strange Orchid," etc. 303pp. 5⅜ × 8½. (Available in U.S. only)
21531-8 Pa. $4.95

AMERICAN SAILING SHIPS: Their Plans and History, Charles G. Davis. Photos, construction details of schooners, frigates, clippers, other sailcraft of 18th to early 20th centuries—plus entertaining discourse on design, rigging, nautical lore, much more. 137 black-and-white illustrations. 240pp. 6⅛ × 9¼.
24658-2 Pa. $5.95

ENTERTAINING MATHEMATICAL PUZZLES, Martin Gardner. Selection of author's favorite conundrums involving arithmetic, money, speed, etc., with lively commentary. Complete solutions. 112pp. 5⅜ × 8½.   25211-6 Pa. $2.95

THE WILL TO BELIEVE, HUMAN IMMORTALITY, William James. Two books bound together. Effect of irrational on logical, and arguments for human immortality. 402pp. 5⅜ × 8½.   20291-7 Pa. $7.50

THE HAUNTED MONASTERY and THE CHINESE MAZE MURDERS, Robert Van Gulik. 2 full novels by Van Gulik continue adventures of Judge Dee and his companions. An evil Taoist monastery, seemingly supernatural events; overgrown topiary maze that hides strange crimes. Set in 7th-century China. 27 illustrations. 328pp. 5⅜ × 8½.   23502-5 Pa. $5.95

CELEBRATED CASES OF JUDGE DEE (DEE GOONG AN), translated by Robert Van Gulik. Authentic 18th-century Chinese detective novel; Dee and associates solve three interlocked cases. Led to Van Gulik's own stories with same characters. Extensive introduction. 9 illustrations. 237pp. 5⅜ × 8½.
23337-5 Pa. $4.95

Prices subject to change without notice.
Available at your book dealer or write for free catalog to Dept. GI, Dover Publications, Inc., 31 East 2nd St., Mineola, N.Y. 11501. Dover publishes more than 175 books each year on science, elementary and advanced mathematics, biology, music, art, literary history, social sciences and other areas.